# Self-Love for Teen Girls

---

*Stop Seeking External Validation, Boost Your Self-Esteem, and Create Your Best Life*

Grace Parker

# Table of Content

# Introduction

*"I feel inadequate when I look in the mirror."*

*"I can't shake off the feeling that I'm just not enough."*

*"I'm afraid to speak my mind because I'm scared no one will understand me."*

*"I struggle to accept my flaws, both physical and emotional."*

*"I often wonder if people truly value me for who I am."*

*"I don't know how to find the inner strength to love myself."*

Do you recognize yourself in these feelings?

Imagine a morning like any other: you wake up, look in the mirror, and only notice the imperfections reflected there. You ask yourself why you can't feel as beautiful as other girls, or why every attempt to appreciate yourself seems to fail. At school, during break, you watch groups of friends laughing and sharing secrets while you struggle to find the right words, afraid no one will listen or understand. It almost seems like other girls have a secret for appearing confident, strong, and at ease, while you constantly feel torn between wanting to be noticed and fearing you won't fit in.

Maybe you've felt that tightness in your stomach when scrolling through social media photos: you see everyone looking so perfect, smiling, and happy, and you wonder why you can't feel that same positive energy inside yourself. Perhaps you've had afternoons when, despite having things to do and people around you, you felt deeply alone, trapped by that inner voice whispering that you're not good enough, that there's nothing special about you. It's that voice that makes you think you need to change, to be different, just to deserve affection, respect, or simply a bit of peace.

If these thoughts and feelings resonate with you, know that you're not alone. Many girls experience this silent pain: a sense of inadequacy and vulnerability born from the fear of not measuring up, from the insecurity of showing who you really are, and from the doubt that you can't accept yourself with all your unique shades and imperfections. This book is here to face that pain with you, to help you recognize it, and to guide you on a journey toward understanding, acceptance, and, ultimately, self-love.

Now imagine a different future. One afternoon, you're in your room and instead of turning away from your reflection in the mirror, you choose to look at it with fresh eyes. You notice your features, the way your eyes catch the light, the subtle details that make your face unique. It's no longer about chasing perfection, but about uncovering the hidden harmony in your own authenticity. In that moment, you begin to sense a kind of peace, as if something inside you is loosening. The tension of having to be someone else, of having to measure up to an unreachable ideal, starts to fade away.

The following day, when you're with your friends, you no longer feel the need to constantly compare yourself to them. Instead, you find yourself laughing and sharing your opinions openly, without fear, because you know your worth doesn't hinge on anyone else's approval. You can be honest, imperfect, and vulnerable without feeling inadequate. By showing who you are, in all your uniqueness, you discover that the people around you actually appreciate those very qualities you once thought were flaws or limitations.

Continuing on this path, social media may no longer serve as a distorted mirror for comparison, but as a space where you can find inspiration, connecting with other girls who, like you, are learning to embrace themselves and appreciate who they are. Rather than feeling uncomfortable in your own body or doubtful about your opinions, you'll begin to experience a sense of empowerment—an uplifting, positive energy that supports you through life's challenges.

Imagine what it feels like to wake up finally comfortable in your own skin, with the inner strength to say, "I am worthy, I deserve this, I belong to myself," without the anxious weight of wondering who you should be. This is the pleasure that comes from cultivating self-love: a sense of calm, of independence, of genuine self-esteem that leads to more authentic relationships, a clearer vision of your future, and the ability to face life with courage and compassion, both for yourself and for others. This is the goal your journey toward self-love can help you reach.

In this book, you'll discover how to turn that negative inner dialogue into a more compassionate and encouraging voice. I'll show you how to recognize limiting thoughts and replace them with positive statements, how to train your mind to focus on your strengths rather than your weaknesses. I'll guide you through practical exercises, tips, and concrete strategies to help you appreciate your body, your emotions, your human qualities, and your uniqueness.

You'll learn how to set healthy boundaries in your relationships, how to express your feelings without fear, and how to find balance between giving and receiving. I'll provide you with simple, clear tools to boost your self-esteem, nurture self-respect, and protect your individuality in a world that often seems to tell you to be different.

Step by step, you'll learn to transform your vulnerability into strength, your insecurities into opportunities for growth. By the end of these pages, my goal is for you to feel that you have the inner resources to love yourself unconditionally, face challenges with greater confidence, and write your personal story with the conviction that you are worthy, you matter, and you deserve a place of genuine respect in your own life.

My name is Grace Parker, and I grew up all too familiar with the feeling of never being truly "enough." I still remember those afternoons of my adolescence when I looked in the mirror and saw only what was wrong, or those moments when I felt I didn't have a real, authentic voice of my own. I was convinced I was the only one who felt such insecurities. It was only as I grew older and spoke with other girls and women that I realized just how widespread that sense of inadequacy was—and how it could be turned into a source of strength.

Over the years, I studied psychology and devoted myself to understanding the inner workings of self-esteem, self-care, and emotional well-being. I listened to the stories of many adolescents— some looking for guidance, others just hoping for a bit of light to find their way through their feelings. Through my work with them, I noticed recurring patterns: fears, limiting beliefs, the anxiety of having to live up to everyone else's expectations. And above all, I saw how, with the right strategies, this pattern can be reversed and transformed into genuine self-appreciation.

This book was born from these very experiences, from my studies, and from truly listening to the voices of girls like you. I'm not here to teach you some abstract theory or to offer you magical formulas devoid of context. Instead, I want to provide you with practical, understandable tools, grounded in evidence and experience, that will help you face the challenges of growing up and view yourself with greater kindness. I'm not your teacher, nor do I wish to place myself on a pedestal; think of me more as a guide, a fellow traveler. What I share in these pages is the result of a journey I've taken as well, and my hope is that, as you read, you'll feel understood, inspired, and free to forge your own path toward self-love.

This is a practical guide designed to help you recognize your worth and develop your self-esteem, beginning with who you are, with the emotions you feel and the experiences you're living right now. It's filled with simple, applicable tools, reflections, and concrete exercises aimed at anyone who wants to stop feeling inadequate and start seeing themselves with more loving eyes.

This isn't a manual for perfection; it's not a list of rigid rules or a collection of theories disconnected from reality. You won't find any magic formulas or unrealistic promises here: I'm not going to tell you that after reading these pages, life will be obstacle-free or that every insecurity will suddenly vanish without a trace. On the contrary, this book is not about teaching you to be someone else, but about discovering the value of being exactly who you are. It's not a text meant to turn you into a stranger to yourself, but a tool to bring you back home—to you—imbued with a new sense of respect, dignity, and love for your uniqueness.

Now that you've grasped the essence of the journey we're about to embark on—moving from deeply rooted insecurities to the attainment of true self-love—it's time to dive into the heart of this path. In the next chapter, we'll begin working on the foundation of every inner transformation: awareness. Through examples, activities, and concrete reflections, you'll start to understand how your inner dialogue works and how you can reshape it to foster a healthier, kinder relationship with the most important person in your life: yourself.

So let's take the first step. Welcome to this journey toward understanding, acceptance, and the celebration of who you truly are. Let's enter the first chapter together.

# Chapter 1:
# Silencing the Negative Inner Voice

*"Talk to yourself like you would to someone you love."* – *Brené Brown*

Imagine standing in front of a classmate who quietly criticizes every move you make. You stumble over a word? She whispers that you're not good enough. You try a new sport? She smirks, convinced you'll fail before you even begin. Now ask yourself: how long would you allow this presence to follow you around, undermining your confidence and your peace of mind?

If you think about it, you might realize this companion sometimes exists only in your own head, a persistent, stern commentator lodging itself in your mind and insisting you're never enough. Maybe you've inherited this voice from past experiences, from others' judgments, or from unaddressed insecurities. Yet this voice doesn't speak the truth; it's merely the echo of distorted beliefs and limiting notions.

In this chapter, you'll explore the roots of these toxic thoughts and learn to recognize them as just a few out-of-tune voices, not infallible judges. Through concrete insights and practical strategies, you can begin transforming that negative buzz into a kinder, more open, and genuinely helpful inner dialogue. It's an important first step toward building a more supportive relationship with yourself, one that lifts you up rather than brings you down. Now let's dig deeper into this dark root and see how to grasp it so you can finally let it go.

## The Roots of Toxic Thoughts

When you start paying close attention to the voice in your head, you might notice it doesn't just emerge out of nowhere. Often, those harsh comments and lingering doubts take root over time, shaped by past experiences and moments of emotional vulnerability. Sometimes they stem from faded memories, fleeting remarks made by someone you cared about, or subtle gestures and expressions you interpreted as definitive proof of your inadequacy. Gradually, these fragments settle in your mind, forming an invisible layer of unexamined beliefs.

Think about how certain negative observations you heard years ago can suddenly resurface when you attempt something new. Maybe your mother, on a tense day, sighed while looking at your grades, leaving you with the impression she was disappointed. Or perhaps a friend made a joke about your appearance, and you turned it into an absolute truth about yourself. These impressions have the power to blur reality, turning a simple passing comment into a permanent label. Without careful reflection, you risk accepting them as factual judgments rather than the fleeting, distorted opinions they really are.

At the core of these toxic thoughts, you'll often find a buildup of unaddressed insecurities. Perhaps you never had the chance to voice your fears, or maybe you never found a safe environment where you could say, "I don't feel good enough." That unspoken emotion then crystallized into a hostile inner message that echoes whenever something goes wrong. This voice doesn't reflect the real world; it emerges from a lack of honest dialogue, from missed opportunities to acknowledge and comfort your more vulnerable side.

In its own way, your mind tries to shield you from pain, warning you of potential failures or humiliations. But in doing so, it sometimes forgets to show compassion. Instead of suggesting, "Be cautious, but you can handle this," it opts for the brutal, "You'll never make it." This pattern is learned, a style you've internalized to manage fear, shame, or disappointment. By calmly observing where these voices originate, you'll see they're more closely tied to a distorted view of past events than to your actual abilities.

Understanding the roots of toxic thoughts demands courage. You need to pause and ask yourself where these ideas come from, who introduced them into your mind, and when they began to take shape. This kind of introspection won't erase those voices overnight, but it does strip away much of their influence. As you recognize their origin, it becomes easier to separate them from who you truly are, seeing them for what they are: echoes of old fears, reflections of distant memories, not your genuine truth.

**Recognizing Harmful Mental Patterns**

Your negative inner voice doesn't always come at you with direct insults or glaring judgments. Sometimes it slips into subtler forms — familiar, steady murmurs that chip away at your abilities or blow small setbacks out of proportion. These aren't just random occurrences; they're ingrained habits of thought, patterns you rely on to interpret the world. If at some point a single bad experience convinced you that you weren't good enough, you might keep returning to that same conclusion, filtering every new situation through it and ignoring any evidence to the contrary.

Take a moment to spot these patterns. If you often generalize, for example, one misstep might make you think, "I messed up that assignment, so I'll never be good at anything." It's like one stain on a page making you believe the entire notebook is ruined. Or maybe you catastrophize, picturing the worst possible outcome from a minor setback, as if a small difficulty at school must mean a total collapse of your life. You might also downplay every success. Even when you achieve something, you tell yourself it was just luck or that you didn't really deserve it, overlooking all the hard work you poured into it.

Recognizing these mental patterns takes patience. Start by observing your daily thoughts. When facing a challenge, how do you interpret it? Do you immediately tear yourself down or assume it will end in disaster? When someone pays you a compliment, what's your knee-jerk response? Do you accept it gratefully, or do you dismiss it as an over-the-top kindness? By noticing how you react, you begin to see the telltale signs of a dysfunctional pattern.

This isn't about constantly debating with yourself, but about becoming aware. Instead of ignoring or enduring negative thoughts, pause and listen closely to what they're saying. Ask yourself: Is this conclusion supported by solid facts, or is it based on hasty interpretations? Do you genuinely have proof, or are you relying on an impossibly strict standard? Often, you'll find that your internal judgments are rooted in isolated events, irrational fears, or some overly idealized vision of who you "should" be.

Recognizing the pattern means understanding that it isn't a life sentence, but a bad habit. Just as you can unlearn a gesture you've been repeating for ages, you can let go of these mental shortcuts. When you spot them, they lose their invisible grip, and you gain more freedom in how you evaluate yourself and your experiences. This doesn't mean you'll never feel negativity again; it means you'll learn to put it in perspective, tone it down, and gradually replace it with a more balanced narrative. This new clarity brings you another step closer to a more honest, supportive inner dialogue—one that helps, rather than hinders, your growth.

## Distinguishing External from Internal Criticism

Often, your negative inner voice doesn't spring up out of thin air. It feeds on judgments that came from outside you. A harsh comment, a disapproving look, or a phrase uttered at a tense moment can settle into your mind. Initially, these are someone else's words, but over time, your inner dialogue starts amplifying them, repeating them insistently. In this way, even a single offhand remark turns into a constant, internal accusation.

Picture an external criticism like a pebble tossed into a pond. The impact creates ripples that expand outward: at first, it's just another person's opinion, but then your inner voice magnifies it, adding new details until it becomes absolute truth. In this process, you forget it began as someone else's idea. Often, the person who made the comment doesn't truly know you, or was reacting under stress, or never thought about the effect their words might have. Yet, in your mind, it all hardens into an undeniable verdict.

The key is learning to separate what others say from how you interpret it. Consider this: an opinion belongs to the person who expressed it, not to you. If someone calls you "incompetent" in a heated moment, it doesn't mean you actually are. Maybe you made a mistake, sure, but that slip-up doesn't define your entire worth. The problem arises when your inner voice picks up that criticism and plays it on loop, erasing all the evidence that proves your abilities. It's as if that voice keeps saying, "They saw something real in me, so I must be exactly that." But that's a hasty conclusion, since you're taking one viewpoint and turning it into your identity.

It helps to pause before accepting a judgment as truth. Ask yourself: who said those words? How well do they know your story, your efforts, your achievements? Is it someone who respects you, or a person who criticizes everyone indiscriminately? Answering these questions can help you put that criticism in perspective and assign it a fair weight. This doesn't mean ignoring all constructive feedback— useful suggestions are part of personal growth. But there's a difference between helpful input and a harsh sentence that ignores your complexity.

Keep in mind that your inner voice should process information to help you understand, not tear you down. If someone points out a mistake, you can note the feedback and consider ways to improve. You don't need to brand yourself a "failure" or "incompetent." The difference between external and internal criticism lies in your ability to filter what comes from outside and separate the comment from who you truly are. This filter prevents every judgment you hear from pouring into your internal dialogue, sparing your self-esteem unnecessary wounds and making room for a more balanced assessment of your real worth.

## Turning Self-Criticism into Strength

Once you start noticing the patterns behind your inner voice, you can take it a step further. Don't just recognize it—try to change its tone. This doesn't mean erasing every negative thought, which wouldn't be realistic. Instead, it's about learning to speak to yourself in a different, more constructive way, much like you would with someone you care about and respect. Each time you catch yourself being overly harsh, pause and ask: would I use the same words with a friend facing a similar struggle?

Imagine, for example, that you've made a mistake. Your first instinct might be to tell yourself, "You're not capable, you failed again." At that very moment, try to intervene. Look at that thought as if it wasn't yours—like a note left behind by someone you don't know. Then replace it with different, more realistic words: "I made a mistake this time, but I can learn and improve." You're not trying to fool yourself by pretending everything is perfect, nor are you denying the importance of what happened. You're simply reminding yourself that one setback does not define your worth, and that there's room to grow.

It helps to cultivate positive statements that feel believable. Avoid overly optimistic phrases that might sound hollow. Instead, choose balanced reminders, such as: "I have strengths I can rely on," "I'm learning to handle these situations better," or "I can do my best and see what happens." Their power lies in their honesty: they acknowledge challenges without being crushed by them. They serve as a prompt that, even if you sometimes forget, you have valuable resources within you.

Being kind to yourself isn't a luxury; it's a practical way to stay clear-headed. Speaking to your mind with compassion eases inner tension.

A supportive tone makes it easier to see situations from a broader perspective and make thoughtful decisions. Fierce self-criticism, on the other hand, limits your chances of finding useful solutions by trapping you in guilt and frustration.

Learning to reframe negative thoughts is a continuous exercise. At first, it might feel strange to swap hostile phrases for understanding ones, almost like you're forcing the conversation. Over time, though, it'll start to feel more natural. You'll discover that your mind can become an ally instead of a relentless judge. Rather than telling yourself you're not good enough, you might say: "I'm not sure how this will go, but I can try. I've overcome challenges before, and this time I can prepare more effectively."

In this way, self-criticism transforms from an obstacle into motivating energy. Instead of knocking you down, it encourages you to improve, to believe a bit more in your abilities, and to give yourself the chance to grow, one step at a time.

# Chapter 2:
# Stop Caring What People Think

*"Be yourself; everyone else is already taken." – Oscar Wilde*

A 2018 study published in the *Journal of Youth and Adolescence* found that a large number of teenagers feel constant pressure to conform to the expectations of their social environment. It's as if every step you take is viewed through the lens of rules you never chose yourself: what you should study, how you ought to dress, what goals you should chase. Each external suggestion nudges you in the same direction, gradually pulling you away from your deepest nature and genuine desires.

This chapter will help you figure out what truly matters to you. By focusing on what you feel—rather than on what others say you ought to do—you can begin loosening the grip these influences have on you. Over time, you'll gain clarity: where does someone else's thinking end and your own begin? Which parts of your life were handed down by others, and which ones did you choose for yourself? The answers will create room for your inner voice, freeing it from those who would rather see you become someone else.

## Identifying the Invisible Weights

Take a moment to look at your decisions. You might notice a hidden thread linking what you do to what others expect of you. Maybe you accepted a particular course of study because it was "the smart choice," without ever asking if it truly excited you. Maybe you spend time with people who don't reflect who you are, just to avoid appearing unsociable. Maybe you've adopted an image you don't believe in, because you're afraid of how others might judge you.

Start recognizing these invisible weights one by one. Begin with the simplest choices: a hobby that doesn't thrill you, a group of friends that leaves you feeling empty, a goal you pursued without any real enthusiasm. Ask yourself: without that suggestion, without that nudge, would I have made the same decision? If the answer is "no," you've just discovered an external expectation that's shaping your path.

Each time you find one of these weights, ask where it comes from. A parent's comment? A persistent teacher's advice? A classmate who always has an opinion about your looks or your interests? Pinpointing the source helps you understand what you once took at face value. Once you notice it, you can choose: continue down that road, or pause and consider options that align better with who you are.

Spotting these invisible weights is an exercise in clarity. It helps you separate what's truly meaningful from what's merely clutter, freeing space for what you genuinely feel. Whenever you recognize an external weight, you loosen a binding force, let in more fresh air, and discover what fuels you. Over time, you'll bridge the gap between what you truly want and what you actually do, moving forward on a path that lines up with your own aspirations. This is where your freedom begins.

**Saying "No" Without Guilt**

Aligning your commitments with what you consider important often depends on your ability to draw clear boundaries. These boundaries frequently emerge when you speak a simple yet powerful word: "no." It can feel intimidating because you worry about disappointing someone or appearing ungrateful. Still, learning to say "no" is essential for protecting your integrity and well-being.

What makes uttering this short word challenging is the sense of guilt that might accompany it. If you've been taught to be accommodating, to never turn others down, you may believe that "no" is a sign of selfishness. But when you accept requests that don't feel true to you, you're taking time and energy away from what genuinely matters. Each "yes" you offer just to please someone else creates an invisible imbalance—a quiet betrayal of your own priorities.

To move forward, start by being honest with yourself. Think of every new request as an object to be evaluated: do you have enough space on your personal "shelf" to add it? If it doesn't match your interests, align with your values, or takes away resources from activities that genuinely resonate with you, it deserves to be declined. This clarity helps you see "no" not as an injury to others, but as an act of care for your inner agenda.

You don't need long or complicated explanations. A sincere refusal can be expressed in a few words: "I appreciate your offer, but I can't right now." You can add a brief note of understanding, but there's no need to justify every detail. Showing respect for others doesn't mean disregarding yourself. Instead, it means communicating in a kind yet firm way. The person in front of you will sense your decision is clear, leaving less room for misunderstandings.

If you still feel uneasy, remember that saying "no" does not destroy genuine relationships. The people who truly value you will understand, or at least accept, your choice. Some may react with surprise or disappointment, but that reveals more about their expectations than any wrongdoing on your part. You're simply restoring balance, putting your life in order. Over time, by regularly declining requests that clash with your priorities, you'll create an environment that's more aligned with who you are.

Consider starting small. Begin with less demanding situations—an invitation to an activity you don't enjoy or a favor you have no desire to fulfill. As you get used to protecting your boundaries, it will feel natural to refuse more significant requests. Gradually, this practice turns "no" from a source of guilt into a tool for balance. Slowly, you'll realize that your time and energy have value, and defending them means honoring what truly matters to you.

Saying "no" without guilt isn't an act of selfishness, but of authenticity. Removing what doesn't belong to you makes room for what genuinely helps you grow. In this way, "no" becomes a tool for making your life more meaningful.

## Disconnecting from Social Judgment

Consider the everyday choices you make, even the smallest ones: the way you pick out your clothes, how you present yourself at school, the afternoon activities you choose to pursue. It might feel as though each action naturally flows from who you are. Yet, behind these decisions often lies the fear of being judged. The society around you is quick to voice its opinions about everything—how you should look, who you should spend time with, what kind of results you should achieve. This constant flow of assessments creates an atmosphere in which other people's judgments become a yardstick you work hard to measure up to.

Pause for a moment and ask yourself: how much room are you giving to social judgment in guiding your choices? When you select an outfit or decide what to say in a conversation, how often do you picture others' reactions? Becoming aware of this dynamic is like turning on a light in a dimly lit room. Suddenly, you notice where you've been adjusting your behavior without even realizing it. Recognizing this doesn't call for guilt; it calls for honest curiosity. The goal is to understand how much the desire to please the crowd affects what you do.

Once you recognize this pattern, you can start to change it. Outside opinions seem significant because you've been letting them in without filters. Try viewing them for what they really are: partial points of view rooted in other people's experiences and biases. Many individuals simply repeat common ideas without ever asking themselves if those ideas truly make sense for you. Learning to disconnect from social judgment means practicing selective listening. You can still hear what people say, but you decide what weight their words carry.

You don't have to withdraw from the world or ignore all advice. Instead, treat opinions as information, not commands. Ask yourself: does this criticism or expectation align with what I genuinely want in my life? Or does it clash with my own values and interests? As you become more aware of your power to filter others' judgments, those that are shallow or driven by envy lose their hold on you. This isn't about closing the door on the outside world; it's about learning to separate helpful influences from those that drag you down.

Disconnecting from social judgment involves building a stable inner core. When you trust in the value of your ideas, you feel less need for constant external approval. This inner stability takes time to develop, but it grows stronger each time you recognize the weight of someone else's opinion and choose not to let it sway you. Over time, you'll find that the world keeps offering opinions, but you won't feel compelled to comply automatically. At the center of your decisions will be your own voice—a more reliable guide, since it's rooted in your true aspirations. By choosing this path, you reduce the impact of social pressures that try to mold you into someone you're not, and open up space for decisions that reflect your authenticity.

## Choosing Authentic Personal Values

If you're wondering why certain choices fail to bring you satisfaction, you might discover that you've been traveling along a track set by others. Personal values work like internal coordinates, guiding your decisions toward what truly matters to you. Defining them isn't just a theoretical exercise; it's a practical tool to set your own course apart from the countless paths others suggest.

Picture yourself pausing in a quiet room, far from the noise of outside opinions. From that calmer vantage point, ask yourself: which aspects of life do I genuinely consider important? Maybe you yearn for sincere relationships, seek ways to express your creativity without restraint, or want to commit your time and effort to causes you believe in. Writing these priorities down brings them out of the vague background and gives them a clear shape.

You don't need a long list. Focus on a handful of solid, honestly chosen points. Each authentic value provides a reason to move in a certain direction. For example, if you realize that the freedom to explore is essential to you, you can weigh every new opportunity in its light. Does this choice move you closer to a more open and curious life, or does it lock you into a rigid path?

Aligning actions and values leads to a profound sense of coherence. When you act in harmony with what you believe in, you discover a kind of peace that's hard to find if you're just following someone else's instructions. You don't have to prove anything to anyone; you're simply living in alignment with your thoughts and feelings. While this doesn't eliminate obstacles, it reduces the feeling that you're fighting for something that isn't yours. Even your toughest efforts take on greater meaning when they fit with your underlying principles.

Choosing authentic personal values doesn't mean isolating yourself from others or rejecting every suggestion. It means having an internal filter that helps you discern. Advice can be useful, but it doesn't define who you are unless it resonates with your principles. The pressure to follow the crowd carries less weight because you know where you're headed. Instead of navigating in the dark, seeking approval, you move forward guided by a map drawn from your deepest sense of self.

Over time, you might revisit those notes to ensure you're staying true to the values you've chosen. You might add new ones or let go of some that no longer feel right. This flexibility doesn't contradict the solidity of your foundation; rather, it allows it to evolve with you. Each time

23

you recalibrate your core points, you sharpen your ability to recognize what truly drives your growth.

Choosing authentic personal values is an act of clarity. It helps you separate what's essential from what's unnecessary, understanding what deserves your energy and what you should leave behind. These internal coordinates become a compass that guides you toward a more integrated life, where your choices reflect who you are, not who others would have you become.

# Chapter 3:
## Discover Your Authentic Self

*"Imperfections are not inadequacies; they are reminders that we're all in this together." – Brené Brown*

Did you know that many people considered "perfect" admit to feeling incomplete when they're alone with their thoughts? In a crowded room, everyone conceals insecurities and moments of uncertainty, even those who appear to have every detail under control. The perfection you admire in others—or that you try so hard to achieve—is often built on a partial image, a careful selection of what's shown to the world. Yet that idealized model doesn't exist in everyday life. Instead of making you feel safer, it pushes you to chase an impossible goal.

In this chapter, you'll learn to dismantle the idol of perfection—an illusory finish line that drains your energy without offering anything truly valuable in return. You'll discover why freeing yourself from this pressure helps reveal your most authentic side. Rather than suffocating rules and arbitrary standards, you'll find the strength to embrace your own characteristics, seeing even your flaws as signs of a fully lived life. Once you're no longer weighed down by that stifling ideal, you can uncover a more solid, natural authenticity—a real foundation for growing your inner confidence.

## Dismantling the Idol of Perfection

Picture yourself holding a pristine notebook: its cover spotless, its pages unblemished, each line flawless and waiting as if for the perfect moment. You regard it with a kind of reverence, afraid that a single crooked mark might ruin it forever. And so you never write a word, endlessly postponing that project or reflection you've long wanted to put down on paper.

Ask yourself: where does the idea come from that this notebook must remain immaculate? Maybe you've absorbed the belief that everything needs to be in perfect order and under control before you even begin, free of any imperfections. You look at people who never seem to falter and imagine their lives unfolding without a hitch, without a stray ink blot. But stop and think: do they truly never make mistakes, or do they simply show the world only their polished outcomes, hiding all their erasures and second thoughts?

The pursuit of perfection leads you to hesitate in front of a blank page, too scared to mar it with anything less than flawless. You avoid new activities, genuine relationships, or challenging opportunities for fear of leaving a flawed mark on that spotless paper. In the end, you produce nothing real, leaving no trace of your creativity or your effort. You remain stuck, paralyzed by the fear of failure, and lose the chance to learn and grow through real experience.

Reverse that mindset: consider every smudge, every awkward attempt as the early lines of a story still unfolding. Rather than avoiding writing in the notebook, see the blank page as an invitation to act, knowing that mistakes don't diminish your worth—they add to the narrative you're creating. When you abandon the idol of perfection, the ink you withheld out of fear begins to flow freely, giving shape to projects and ideas uniquely your own.

Instead of endlessly delaying that first stroke, pick up the pen and begin. Those smudges will be signs of your journey, not proof of irreversible failure. Each imperfection is a starting point for improvement, a reminder that you're learning and evolving. In time, your notebook will fill up with notes, corrections, and underlines, making it one-of-a-kind and alive. It may never be "perfect" in some abstract sense, but it will have a story, depth, and human richness.

Dismantling the idol of perfection means freeing yourself from the need to be impeccable. You let go of that pristine image that, in truth, holds you back from taking any steps at all. You accept that you'll leave a few ink stains, that some lines will be crooked, that you might pick the wrong word now and then—and that's okay, as long as it's your path, defined by tangible actions rather than unattainable ideals. In this new approach, your identity is no longer tethered to an untouchable standard. Instead, it's shaped day by day through your choices, your attempts, and your genuine efforts. The anxiety of keeping the notebook pristine fades, replaced by the satisfaction of watching your authenticity emerge, line by imperfect line.

## Celebrating Imperfections

Think about it for a moment: if every object, every person, and every experience in your life were perfectly symmetrical and flawless, the world would look as flat as a landscape drawn with a ruler. Everything would be predictable, repetitive, lacking that spark that makes each moment distinct. Imperfections, on the other hand, add depth, character, and authenticity. All it takes is paying attention to realize that it's often the flaws that make something worth remembering.

Consider a friend whose honesty you appreciate, even when they don't say exactly what you'd like to hear. Maybe sometimes their words are a bit blunt, or their manner slightly rough around the edges. Yet precisely because they're not hiding anything, this person feels more real, closer, and truer to life. They're not acting out some ideal version of what a friend "should" be; they're an authentic individual, with sharp angles and corners to discover. Their imperfections remind you that they're living their truth, not following a script.

Apply this same perspective to your own life, and you'll notice that you often remember most fondly the moments when things didn't go exactly as planned. Maybe it was a trip where you missed your train and had to stop in a town you'd never heard of, stumbling upon a hidden café you never would have found had everything gone "smoothly." Or the time your project ran behind schedule, forcing you to improvise a more creative solution. Those little detours created unexpected situations and gave you unique lessons and memories.

Celebrating imperfections doesn't mean settling for mediocre results. Rather, it shifts the focus from trying to avoid every flaw to embracing the human element they represent. If you focus too much on achieving an ideal standard, you risk missing out on the experience itself. Imperfections signal that you're learning something, experimenting, and shaping your life through trial, correction, and rediscovery.

Start with small steps: when you notice something isn't perfect, instead of reacting with frustration, pause and consider what's in front of you. Maybe there's a detail that can be improved. Or perhaps it's that very ink stain on a page that makes the text feel more alive. Maybe a miscalculation revealed a fresh angle that enriches your perspective. Every imperfection holds a story and a potential lesson.

This attitude also extends to the way you see yourself. Accepting a physical characteristic that doesn't fit a perfect standard or a personality trait that doesn't meet others' expectations frees you from the weight of external judgment. An imperfection can become not just a sign of uniqueness but a source of strength: your voice, your journey, and your way of living gain depth precisely through the nuances that, at first glance, seem out of line with some ideal model.

Ultimately, celebrating imperfections means recognizing that life isn't an assignment to be completed without errors, but a canvas to fill with all kinds of colors and strokes. There's no need to erase every smudge. Instead, you can admire them as markers of an authentic, unique path that's entirely your own.

## Valuing Your Unique Talents

In your daily life, some abilities show themselves clearly, like your knack for choosing just the right words or your skill in a creative activity. Others hide in seemingly ordinary gestures. Maybe you have a way of putting anyone at ease, a talent for neatly organizing complex information, or a gift for finding quick solutions to practical problems. Each quality draws a unique line in the portrait of who you are.

To appreciate these abilities, pay attention to the moments when your actions flow with ease. Notice the situations that energize you, the ones where your efforts feel natural. This careful observation shines a light on what deserves more room in your life. Identifying these skills adds strength to your decisions and offers a starting point for growth—a chance to refine methods and strategies.

There's no universal standard. Everyone follows their own path. Your strengths are resources you can use to express what you have to offer, creating a positive impact on those around you. A particular ability helps you overcome obstacles, a creative approach opens up new directions, and a practical mindset solves intricate problems.

Valuing a talent means testing it, trying it out in different contexts, experimenting with new tools. If you sense a talent for listening, you can train it by investing time in meaningful conversations. If you notice sparks of creativity, explore unfamiliar territory. Each step makes your competence clearer, more ready to support your goals.

It's enough to appreciate the impact of what you do well. The idea isn't to seek approval from others, but to find a direction aligned with your intentions. When you connect abilities and objectives, your decisions gain consistency. Every milestone reached reinforces your belief that you have what it takes to move forward confidently.

Each unique talent broadens your map of possibilities. It lets you respond to challenges with greater effectiveness, seize unexpected opportunities, and adapt your contributions according to what you consider important. By observing your abilities closely, you choose where to invest them. In this way, your talents take root in your daily life, supporting your journey and providing reliable tools to accomplish what truly matters to you.

## Discovering the Courage to Be Yourself

Remember the last time you talked to a friend without filtering your emotions, letting your voice come through without wondering if it was "right"? Maybe you were sitting on a bench as afternoon slowly melted into evening, and a gentle silence welcomed the words you chose so carefully. That feeling of lightness—the absence of any need to please or prove yourself—felt like a breath of fresh air after hours in a closed room.

When you decide to show what you truly feel, you send a clear signal: your essence deserves room to exist. This authenticity brightens your relationships, freeing them from other people's expectations and bringing them closer to genuine dialogue. If a connection still works even after you've revealed sides of yourself that were previously hidden, it means that relationship was never based on masks or scripted roles.

It helps to focus on the values that matter most to you. Ask yourself: which principles guide me? Which qualities do I want to nurture in what I do? Identifying these anchors helps you recognize when a choice aligns with your inner core. Sometimes it's about small gestures: a firm but honest refusal, an opinion voiced without fear, a way of acting that reflects what you truly feel. Every word that aligns with your values strengthens your sense of security.

Examining the fears that sometimes hold you back can show you where to find the strength to move forward. Certain parts of you may remain hidden because you're afraid of judgment or unpredictable reactions. Yet the more you examine these barriers, the more clearly you see where to direct your efforts. Every step toward greater authenticity encourages those around you to do the same. A genuine smile, a sincere remark, a respectful silence—these become pieces of a mosaic where no one feels the need to put on a performance.

Showing yourself as you are doesn't require revealing every thought or emotion. You can share only what feels meaningful to you, letting your voice emerge clearly. An authentic conversation creates stronger bonds, because it reveals the essence of those involved. People who appreciate you discover a chance to know the real you, while those who don't resonate with your truth drift away, leaving room for more compatible connections.

Over time, this sincerity becomes second nature. The urge to fit a mold fades, as does the effort to appear different from who you are. The confidence you gain helps you navigate the world with calm, recognizing your right to exist as you are, without masks or the pretense of perfection. Being yourself gives oxygen to your choices and lets the best of you emerge. In this more authentic flow, you feel a freedom that encourages you to grow and connect with those who value the real person, not the shadow of circumstance.

# Chapter 4:
# Building Self-Esteem

*"No one can make you feel inferior without your consent." –*
*Eleanor Roosevelt*

Have you ever wondered why it's so easy to see the strengths in the people around you, yet the image you have of yourself often seems faded, distant, and hard to grasp? Think about when you watch a friend succeed at something: you clearly recognize her talent, sense her strength, admire her ability to handle challenging situations. Yet, when it's your turn to tap into your own potential, something shifts. It's as if you're staring at a blank page, as though the keen eye that usually spots subtle qualities and hidden strengths no longer knows where to look. This chapter aims to guide you in taking that crucial step: learning to identify the "bricks" that make up your self-esteem, acknowledging the qualities you already possess, and appreciating the large or small successes you've achieved. In doing so, the confidence you have in yourself becomes solid ground to stand on, without having to wait for anyone else's approval to feel worthy.

## Identifying Your Distinctive Qualities

When you look into the mirror of your own mind, you risk focusing only on the dark corners. It's as if your attention always falls on the flaws in the final outcome, ignoring the skill, effort, and resourcefulness it took to get there. Yet many of your strengths live in the everyday gestures often hidden within situations you don't even consider remarkable. Maybe you're truly a good listener, going beyond just words to tune into a friend's emotions. Or perhaps you have a knack for organization, finding order where everyone else sees only chaos. Maybe your imagination can give color and shape to ideas that remain blurry for others.

You tend to underestimate these qualities because, to you, they feel "natural," immediate, woven into the fabric of who you are. They don't seem special—just the way you usually do things. But right there, in those abilities you handle with ease, lie powerful resources: they can support you when obstacles appear, push you to create solutions others can't see, and help you stand out where everyone else blends in.

To spot them, try thinking of moments when you've felt useful and steady. When was the last time you solved a small household problem without slipping into complaints? When did you reassure someone sad with just the right, sincere, comforting words? When have you managed to juggle your time between studying, hobbies, and rest, without giving up on what truly nurtures you? Each time you discover an area where you feel confident, you're getting closer to one of your unique strengths.

They don't have to be flashy talents worthy of the spotlight. Often, the most valuable traits remain submerged until you decide to shine a light on them. It's a quiet inventory, a private exploration that reveals skills, leanings, and aptitudes. Every discovery should be recorded— not as a dry list of merits, but as a map of strengths you can draw from when you need them. Finding these qualities doesn't mean puffing out your chest to brag; it means cultivating a more honest inner dialogue, one that reminds you of what you're good at. This step marks the beginning of a path toward a self-esteem built on tangible, genuinely yours, and truly solid foundations.

**Building a Solid Base of Self-Esteem**

Imagine your self-esteem as a wall you build one brick at a time. There's no single action that erects it instantly; it's a series of small steps, repeated over and over. Each time you face a challenge with courage, you place another brick. Each time you recognize your strengths and put them to use, another brick goes up. The process is almost invisible, but it's steady and ongoing.

Think back to a time when you overcame something that once seemed beyond your reach. Maybe you tackled a tough assignment or handled an unexpected twist without losing your cool. In that moment, you weren't just solving a problem; you were laying another foundation stone for your confidence. Take a moment to jot it down somewhere, even in a simple notebook. It doesn't have to be a long list—just a clear, concise record. Later, when you look back, you'll remember that your bricks are already in place.

You don't need heroic feats. Often, the difference is made by everyday accomplishments: managing your time well, helping a friend through a rough patch, finishing a challenging study session. Each detail is another brick added. Keeping track of these moments creates an internal "archive" of genuine proof. It's like having an inner shelter to return to when doubt comes knocking. The more you acknowledge what you've done, the easier it becomes to draw on this reservoir of strength.

This isn't magic—it's habit. Like any other skill, confidence builds by adding small wins and learning to truly see them. Over time, your mind will stop treating self-esteem as a distant ideal and start recognizing it as a solid fact. You're not chasing some abstract concept; you're reinforcing something real and tangible. One brick today, another tomorrow, and eventually you'll have a wall strong enough to support you in any situation.

## Celebrating Achievements as a Daily Habit

Every evening offers a brief window for you to acknowledge what you've accomplished that day. Instead of letting these moments slip by unnoticed, create a simple ritual that brings your successes into clear focus. Think of this as a deliberate pause, one you shape into a comforting habit. There's no need for elaborate tools—just a quiet space and your own voice.

Choose a familiar spot where you feel at ease. Perhaps you'll sit on the edge of your bed or settle into a comfortable chair by a window. Dim the lights, let the day's noise drift away, and take a slow, steady breath. When you're ready, say aloud one or two things that went well. Maybe you completed a task that had been hanging over your head, offered support to a friend in need, or took a step toward a goal that once felt distant. By naming these successes out loud, you transform them from fleeting thoughts into clearly defined achievements.

This ritual can be as short as a minute or two, yet it gives structure to your reflections. Each time you speak your wins into the quiet room, you affirm their importance. Rather than recording them in a journal, you allow their presence to linger in the air around you. If you'd like an extra layer of meaning, add a small symbolic gesture—light a candle before you begin, or hold a smooth stone in your hand as you speak. Over time, these simple acts become anchors, tying your progress to a tangible practice you can trust.

As you repeat this ritual night after night, a subtle shift occurs. You start looking forward to it because it reinforces a positive narrative about who you are and what you're capable of doing. Moments that might have passed unnoticed now stand out as evidence of your capacity to learn, adapt, and persevere. Instead of relying solely on external praise, you provide recognition for yourself, reinforcing a sense of self-esteem rooted in your own actions.

This habit can influence how you move through the rest of your day, too. Knowing you'll pause to celebrate your progress later may prompt you to seek out opportunities for growth. You won't just wait for big milestones; you'll appreciate the small steps that lead there. In this way, the ritual feeds back into your motivation, guiding you to focus on actions that matter to you.

Over the weeks and months, you'll notice that this simple evening practice has become a stabilizing force. It doesn't have to be dramatic or time-consuming. Its power lies in consistency and sincerity. By continually highlighting what you've done well, you nurture a perspective that values effort, resilience, and personal growth. Before long, you'll find that you stand a bit taller, speak with more conviction, and trust yourself more fully—a natural result of honoring your achievements, day by day.

## Cultivating an Inner Sense of Authority

Your next decision offers a chance to honor your own judgment. Each time you face a choice, consider a brief, meaningful pause before you move forward. Begin with something simple—deciding how to spend a short break, choosing which topic to study first, or selecting an activity to unwind after a long day. Instead of asking a friend, reading a review, or searching for guidance online, slow down and listen to what you already know.

Take one calm breath, then ask yourself: "What do I want from this moment?" Wait a second and notice what comes to mind. Perhaps it's an urge to start a project you've been curious about, or the comfort of revisiting a familiar hobby. Once you sense that direction, follow it. This small act confirms that your internal compass is reliable, that your preferences and insights matter. There's no need to write it down this time. You create a memory in motion, one that exists in the moment you act.

To reinforce this habit, choose a subtle physical cue that accompanies each decision made by your own guidance. Maybe you run your thumb along the edge of a bracelet you wear every day, or gently tap your fingertips together—a small, personal signal that says, "I trust myself here." This touch is quick and unobtrusive, yet it serves as a bridge between your inner reasoning and the steps you take.

Repeat this process throughout your day. With each decision guided by your own instincts, you add another layer of confidence. Over time, these choices form a pattern: you see that you've navigated many small crossroads based on your own understanding. This consistency shapes a mindset that no longer depends on constant confirmation from the outside world. Instead, you welcome input as information to consider, not as the final word.

As your comfort with this approach grows, you'll find that making choices independently feels natural. The space once filled by doubt now holds a quiet certainty. When challenges appear, you won't hesitate as much, because you're used to drawing on your own perspective. This doesn't require dramatic gestures or sweeping changes—just a willingness to practice a new habit, decision by decision.

Eventually, these moments of self-directed action define how you move through life. You'll notice that your voice carries more weight in your own mind. You approach opportunities with clarity, not because someone told you what to do, but because you learned to rely on your internal guidance. The gestures and small pauses blend into your routine, becoming part of who you are. With each choice, you strengthen the link between your intentions and your actions, building self-esteem that stands firm on a foundation you've created for yourself.

# Chapter 5:
# Your Body as a Home

*"Your body is not wrong. Society's expectations are."* – Anonymous

Imagine having a space all your own, a place where you feel safe even when chaos rages outside. It doesn't need to be perfect or luxurious. What matters is that it's welcoming, sturdy, capable of shielding you when the wind roars. Now think of your body. It isn't a piece of clothing you slip into on special occasions, nor a decorative object to be constantly examined. It's your home, and it deserves honest care. In this chapter, you'll learn to look within without rigidity, to recognize the unrealistic standards trying to distort your perception. Once you dismantle the tyranny of imposed ideals, you'll realize that your true strength doesn't hinge on a fixed image, but on the harmony between your authentic sensations and the sincere respect you offer yourself.

## Dismantling Unrealistic Ideals

Imagine a photo on your phone's screen: perfect lighting, vivid colors, every detail meticulously arranged. Behind that image, someone picked the ideal angle, added filters, and discarded dozens of shots. It isn't a spontaneous snapshot; it's the product of careful construction. Now ask yourself: how many times have you measured your own appearance against images engineered to impress? Perhaps you've assumed that what you see sets a standard worth chasing, as if it represented normality.

These ideals operate quietly. Everywhere you look—magazines, ads, social media feeds—you find a visual narrative that seems to lay out unwritten rules. Facial shape, proportions, the slightest detail are presented as benchmarks. No one needs to spell it out: sometimes you absorb these patterns without noticing. Gradually, the natural differences in your body start to seem like oddities. But consider the source: who decided certain features deserve more admiration than others? Why attach greater value to one set of traits?

Look at the mechanism. Your mind processes selective images. A celebrity always shows their best angle; an influencer chooses only carefully curated pictures. This comes across as normal, yet it's really a series of decisions, edits, and filters. Meanwhile, you live in the real world. You wake up with a sleepy face, you walk down the street, you breathe unfiltered air. There's no stage lighting setting the scene. These polished photos don't deny reality, but they shrink it down to a retouched instant.

Keep in mind that true strength lies in understanding what's behind these images. Recognizing the presence of calculated lighting, posed postures, and digital tweaks means no longer mistaking the tip of the iceberg for the whole mountain. You can appreciate the aesthetic care that went into a photo, but there's no need to adopt it as a yardstick for evaluating your reflection. That image freezes a fragment in time; it doesn't represent a person's complexity, let alone yours. You're not looking at an objective fact, but a visual proposal crafted to make an impact.

Try a simple experiment: the next time you encounter a polished photo, consider how many choices shaped that result. Don't just think about the subject's features; consider the lighting, the background, the discarded expressions. Notice there's no fair comparison between your daily life and that glossy fraction of a second. With this perspective, you acknowledge your own complexity, the natural flow of your routines. What you see isn't an enemy; it's a partial representation. This awareness broadens your view, letting you distinguish between visual artifice and living reality.

By doing so, you no longer conform to rigid models. Instead, you recognize life's variety. Instead of feeling inadequate before an unattainable image, you gain a clearer perspective: you see the difference between crafted illusion and authenticity. In that understanding, you find new ways to interpret your appearance without manufactured filters.

## Rewriting Your Relationship with the Mirror

Approach the mirror with a fresh intention. For a few days, turn that everyday encounter into an exercise in active observation. You're not there to hand out compliments or hunt for flaws. Your goal is simply to notice what's present: lines, colors, shapes, expressions. The aim is to minimize judgment and appreciate the act of seeing itself. It's a conversation born from silence, not from automatic commentary.

Before looking, pause. Inhale, exhale, and focus on your breathing. Then lift your gaze slowly. Frame your face as if it were an unfamiliar landscape. Discover subtle details usually overlooked: the curve of your lips at rest, the shape of your eyebrows, the texture of your skin. Observe without seeking meaning. If something catches your eye, acknowledge that it's part of your face today, at this hour, under this light.

Now pick three features of your face that stir a memory, an emotion, or a pleasant feeling. No need for grand achievements: maybe slightly tired eyes remind you of a cozy evening spent reading, or a small mole recalls a past vacation. Perhaps a lock of hair falling in an unexpected way reflects your personality without any special effects. The key isn't judgment; it's linking real elements to lived moments, avoiding invented perfections.

This exercise shifts your focus. Usually, looking in the mirror triggers instant reactions: approval, disappointment, indifference. Now you're applying a different method. You're not searching for a single truth, just observing a reflection in constant flux. Day by day, the image changes. Morning light differs from evening light, your expression shifts with thoughts and feelings. There's no final version of you, only a succession of moments.

If before you lingered on what you considered inadequate, now you experience a wider view. This doesn't mean pretending everything is perfect. It means acknowledging those traits without letting them overshadow the whole picture. You hold a wealth of expressions, micro-movements, and marks that make you recognizable. Your task isn't to rate them, but to register them.

After a week, reflect on any changes. Perhaps negative feelings have softened, or you notice features previously ignored. Maybe you no longer feel compelled to chase an ideal image. Each day you give yourself a chance to see without filtering, to separate observation from criticism. Over time, this approach shapes a new relationship with the mirror: not a judge, but a tool—one that connects you with the present and clarifies that your identity isn't confined to the reflection, but revealed in it as a moving truth.

**Nourishing the Body with Intention**

Think of every meal as an invitation to discover something new about yourself. There's no script, just a palette of flavors to explore. Look around your kitchen and try small changes. Taste a fruit you rarely choose, cook a vegetable differently, experiment with unexpected spices. When you savor food this way, you're not just eating, you're listening to your body's signals.

Before you start eating, pause. Ask yourself: am I hungry or seeking comfort? Craving novelty or longing for reassurance? No answer is wrong. It's a process of understanding. If you want something light, follow that instinct. If a heartier dish appeals, embrace that choice. You're not following mechanical rules; you're creating a dialogue within. This approach doesn't narrow variety; it expands it, turning every decision into a lab where you observe how your body responds, how it feels after a meal, which energies emerge.

Similarly, think of movement as a chance to broaden your range of sensations. No grand feats needed. A walk in a new neighborhood, a few bodyweight exercises, a bike ride with a friend—every movement provides feedback. Your body signals tensions to release, areas awakened by gentle effort, breaths that deepen. Notice if you prefer outdoor activities or a quiet space where you move slowly. The goal isn't performance, but exploration.

Don't chase textbook results. The point is to see how you respond to different stimuli. Maybe try stretching at night and see how it feels in the morning. Observe your energy levels if you adjust recovery times. Experiment with pace and duration. Instead of following rigid formulas, you explore scenarios that reveal who you are and what invigorates you. Each discovery makes your connection with your body more dynamic and inclusive.

Over time, you'll notice clearer preferences. Some flavors leave you feeling light yet satisfied, some activities energize you more than a standard workout. By choosing with intention, you build a personal map. Your body becomes a traveling companion, and each nutritional or movement choice enriches the journey. You're not respecting an external protocol; you're developing a method that grows with you.

This ongoing practice refines your perception. You eat to nourish yourself, discover tastes that speak to your curiosity, move as a way of exploring your limits. If one day you find no new stimuli, that's fine. You can search for others tomorrow. Each gesture trains you to understand internal signals. It's a journey without a fixed destination, guided by your rhythms, emotions, and the immense potential for well-being hidden in simple, curious, and respectful choices.

## Feeling at Ease in Your Own Skin

Imagine your day as a series of small tiles. Each morning, you decide how to dress, how to eat, and how to move. You're not aiming to look a certain way, but to choose actions that improve the quality of your time. A soft sweater on a cool day, comfortable clothes during an afternoon of studying, a pause to breathe deeply. Repeated choices, day after day, build a sense of inner steadiness.

Consider the morning routine: you open your closet and, instead of asking if that garment matches a standard, you wonder how it will make you feel. Warmth, comfort, practicality? This question guides your selection, aligning your decisions with what you genuinely sense. The same applies to movement: stretch a bit after getting up, give yourself a few minutes of gentle exercises. You don't compare yourself to abstract ideals; you pick actions attuned to what you need right now.

Throughout the day, insert simple habits that reinforce the balance between body and mind. A short walk between tasks, a cup of tea enjoyed slowly, a few moments of conscious breathing—these rituals create a stable foundation. They're not chasing a perfect image; they're enhancing your daily experience. Small, meaningful gestures that emerge from tuning in to what you feel.

Over time, these behaviors outline a broader horizon. You find that feeling at ease in your own skin isn't a prize you earn, but a natural result of consistent choices. When you prepare a balanced meal, it's not to meet a rule, but to ensure strength and clarity. When you plan a walk, it's not to obey an external command, but to honor your need to move. It's an ongoing dialogue where each action integrates body and mind more fully.

Notice how these daily attentions influence your self-perception. The pursuit of an ideal form loses importance. Harmony isn't born from conforming to a model, but from choosing actions that match your reality. Each time you tailor the context to your needs, you reinforce your sense of presence. You're not reacting to outside pressures; you're acting in line with what helps you feel good.

Over the long run, these small steps build tangible confidence. You connect with a form of well-being that doesn't depend on comparison or competition. If one day you feel less energetic, you can adjust course, try something different. The key is maintaining the habit of listening to signals and responses. There's no final goal, just a path where you strengthen your bond with your body, making it a trusted reference point in your everyday life.

# Chapter 6:
# Defusing the Influence of Social Media

*"Don't compare your behind-the-scenes to someone else's highlight reel." – Anonymous*

According to a 2018 study by Common Sense Media, teenagers spend several hours a day on social media, scrolling through carefully curated images, videos, and stories. This constant stream of polished content flows across the screen, presenting flawless lives, staggering achievements, and intense emotions. From this unending exposure emerges a quiet form of comparison: your own life, with its regular, ordinary moments, might seem less exciting. It's easy to be enchanted by profiles where everything looks perfect—dream vacations, impeccable style, days packed with success. But how much of reality remains hidden, overshadowed by appearances?

In this chapter, you'll explore how social media influences your perception of yourself and the world around you. You'll learn to select content that truly adds value, setting healthy boundaries and recognizing which information supports your well-being. The goal isn't to demonize these platforms, but to equip yourself with tools that make your online experience consistent with your values and needs. You'll achieve this through awareness: observing how certain images affect your mood, judgment, and self-esteem; understanding that every profile, behind the scenes, filters and chooses what to display.

On a practical level, you'll discover methods to free your self-worth from digital metrics, avoid draining comparisons, and rediscover the importance of offline time. You'll develop a critical approach capable of distinguishing genuine inspiration from invisible pressure. This means filtering content, cutting out toxic influences, and tailoring your feed to reflect a reality closer to your own. You'll realize that you don't need constant approval or relentless comparisons. You have the right to a more balanced relationship with the digital world, one in which external voices don't erode the inner confidence you nurture day after day.

## Filtering Digital Voices

Open a social media platform, and you're met with a constant flow of images, opinions, and suggestions. Some content lifts your mood, while other posts leave you feeling weighed down. How can you quickly distinguish what benefits you from what destabilizes you? A practical strategy is to create a simple "mental filter" before, during, and after using social media.

Start with a short exercise: the next time you open the app, ask yourself three questions. First: "How do I feel right now?" Second: "Why am I logging in at this moment?" Third: "What do I hope to get out of this experience?" Answering honestly helps you set an intention. If you're opening it just out of boredom, you might be more vulnerable to content that adds nothing positive. If you're looking for inspiration on a specific topic, you'll have a better sense of direction.

While browsing, pay attention to your body's reactions. If a post makes you feel anxious, envious, or empty, mentally note that profile. You might jot it down in a notebook or a note-taking app, using a simple code: one symbol for profiles that unsettle you, another for those that energize you. After a few days, you'll have a clear map. You'll see which digital voices spark creativity, serenity, or curiosity, and which ones fuel stress or insecurity.

Another concrete method is to measure short-term effects: after a 10-15 minute session online, stop and rate your emotional state on a scale of 1 to 10. If your rating consistently drops when you follow certain accounts, that's a sign. Maybe it's time to mute or remove them. On the other hand, if certain profiles raise your score, highlight them—

perhaps by creating a "Favorites" folder or saving particularly helpful content.

This isn't about building a bubble devoid of contrasting ideas. Exposure to differing viewpoints can be enriching. The difference lies in quality. A profile that offers constructive insights, even if it critiques aspects of society, can help you grow. One that revolves around sterile comparisons or polished perfection, however, may unsettle you. The goal isn't to avoid differences of opinion, but to identify which ones make you think and which make you feel inadequate without offering any benefit.

If this seems complicated, start small: try removing or muting just one account that negatively affects you. Track the results over a week. Do you feel any improvement? Less tension? More time and energy for what truly interests you? Proceed gradually. This "practical filtering" strategy lets you keep your digital space alive, retaining what nourishes your well-being and reducing the presence of content that erodes your stability. In the end, your feed will reflect a more conscious selection, tuned to your real needs rather than to random standards or social pressure.

## Breaking Free from Virtual Comparison

As you scroll through social media, you often come across lives that seem to run along perfect tracks—sparkling moments, goals achieved effortlessly, happiness displayed with ease. Faced with these images, comparison arises almost instinctively: "Why isn't my life like that?" "Why don't I have their results?" To break this chain, focus on practical tools that make you more aware of the partial nature of these portrayals.

A first step is to schedule an "emotional check" after each social media session. Set a reminder on your phone: after 10-15 minutes of browsing, close the app and note how you feel. Write down a few lines about your mood. Are you sadder, more restless, more insecure? Or maybe indifferent? Doing this consistently links your social media use to the emotions that follow. Soon you'll understand which situations trigger that toxic comparison.

Learn to read between the lines. A profile may showcase spectacular achievements, but you don't see their failures, second thoughts, or abandoned paths. Remember that social media are shop windows, not full documentaries. To internalize this idea, try an exercise: whenever you see a success story, imagine at least three possible behind-the-scenes scenarios you don't see. Maybe that person made countless mistakes before succeeding. Maybe they sacrifice a lot of rest. Maybe they aren't as fulfilled as they seem. This technique doesn't aim to diminish others, but to add depth, reminding you that what you see is a carefully chosen fragment.

Another practical tool is setting your own markers of growth. Instead of comparing yourself to those who seem perfect, define your own indicators. You might decide to measure progress on a skill: improve by one grade in a school subject, learn a new recipe each month, or exercise regularly. Judge yourself against your starting point, not against strangers online. Keep a small record of your steps forward. Whenever you feel comparison creeping in, reread your notes. You'll see progress, effort, and successes crafted for you and you alone.

Also reduce situations that spark useless comparisons: if an account always leaves you feeling behind, consider unfollowing or muting it. You could also limit social media use to times when you feel more emotionally stable—after a walk, or once you've accomplished a task. This way, the impact of comparisons lessens.

Finally, if possible, talk about these feelings with friends. You'll often discover they share similar insecurities. Discussing these difficulties openly helps normalize the sense of "chasing a mirage." With these concrete strategies, virtual comparison loses its grip. It's no longer a constant weight, but a signal to interpret with clarity, reminding you that your path is unique and doesn't rely on unrealistic parallels.

## Setting Healthy Online Boundaries

Defining online boundaries isn't just about saying "no" to excessive social media use. It's about using tools and features to protect your time and mind. Today's devices offer various options to regulate your digital consumption. Take advantage of them to create a more manageable environment.

Start with your phone's settings: most operating systems have a "Screen Time" feature that shows how many hours you spend on apps. Observe it without judgment, then set small goals: reduce your daily time on a platform by 10 minutes, or allow yourself one evening a week without checking social media. Small, steady steps are more effective than drastic, unsustainable attempts.

Explore pause or temporary block functions. Many apps let you set daily limits. For example, you can restrict yourself to 30 minutes on a social platform, after which the app locks automatically. This isn't an impenetrable wall, but a reminder to reflect: "Do I really need to stay here longer?"

Another tool: turn off unnecessary notifications. If every beep distracts you, try allowing alerts only from apps or contacts that truly matter. This removes the "constant call" effect that makes you check your phone every few minutes. With this simple action, you create a kind of virtual silence that gives you space to focus. When you do open a social app, you do so intentionally, not out of reflex.

Consider "usage windows" too. For example, no social media before breakfast or during the hour before bed. You can also use external timers: a simple stopwatch, a productivity app, or even a sticky note on your screen. The key is making your commitments visible. If you promise yourself to stop at 9 p.m., set an alarm. When it rings, close the app without drama. It's training yourself in self-control.

If you want to go further, try "digital fasts": one afternoon a week without a smartphone, a Sunday offline, or an hour a day reading a book instead of scrolling through your feed. You don't have to give up technology entirely, just learn to manage it more flexibly. These experiments show you that life flows smoothly even without constantly monitoring the virtual world.

If it's tough, share your goals with a friend or family member, someone who understands the importance of reducing digital pressure. Making a small commitment public—like limiting social time—can help keep you on track. Every boundary you put in place isn't a sacrifice, but an investment in the quality of your time and attention. By cleverly using tools you already have, you transform your online experience into an option, not an endless obligation.

## Creating a Feed that Inspires

The variety in your feed can be a powerful growth tool. It's not just about adding different colors to your "digital library," but about choosing content that encourages you to develop new skills, interests, and perspectives. Instead of repeating the concept of diversity in abstract terms, consider tangible examples: following science communicators can help you better understand school subjects, emerging artists might inspire you to try a creative hobby, and social activists could spark reflections you bring into the classroom or discussions with friends.

To make this approach effective, set aside a monthly "maintenance" moment for your feed. Note which accounts you've followed recently: which ones prompted you to pick up a book on a new topic? Which encouraged you to research something you studied at school? Write down the concrete results. If you realize a profile positively influenced your learning or ignited creative sparks, keep it. If another leaves you indifferent or even demotivated, don't hesitate to remove it.

Don't stick to the same old sources: explore fields you don't know. Maybe you've never been interested in astronomy, ethnic cuisine, contemporary poetry, or instrumental music. Following a well-curated account on one of these topics might lead you to try something new in real life—attempting an exotic recipe, writing a few lines of poetry, or discovering a local music festival. Your feed thus becomes a springboard for tangible experiences.

Encourage variety in formats too: not just perfect images, but also textual content, podcasts, educational videos. This trains different types of attention and helps you learn in various ways. You'll shift from visual thinking to logical reasoning, from empathetic listening to critical analysis.

Don't be afraid to change your mind. If an account that once inspired you now offers nothing useful, remove it. Your life evolves, your interests shift. A static feed won't reflect your growth. Instead, a flexible, dynamic one becomes a tool to broaden your knowledge. You might even set specific goals: follow a history channel for a month, then delve deeper into a topic it covered by reading a book or visiting a museum.

By doing this, your feed stops being a passive space where you endure random stimuli and becomes a resource that supports your personal development. Every new account you follow, every piece of content you save, every interaction you make creates a path rich in potential. You're no longer just "filtering" to avoid the negative; you're actively building a collection of ideas that can influence how you think, learn, and create—turning your online time into an investment in your future.

# Chapter 7:
# Surrounding Yourself with the Right People

*"Surround yourself with only people who are going to lift you higher." – Oprah Winfrey*

In this chapter, you'll learn to recognize genuine friendships, to understand who truly stands by you and who, instead, undermines your self-esteem. By following clear criteria, you'll discover how to invest your time and energy in those who truly enrich your life.

## Recognizing Genuine Friendships

A few years ago, after a failed school performance, I found myself sitting on a bench behind the gym, shoulders slumped, gaze unfocused. I had just stumbled badly in something I cared about, and I felt absurdly out of place. A classmate I considered a friend shot me a quick, dismissive look and then started talking about something else, ignoring my frustration. The feeling of isolation cut deep: I wondered if the bonds I'd built were too fragile to withstand my moments of weakness.

Right when I was questioning whether I'd always need to hide my uncertainties, another classmate—someone from a parallel class with whom I'd barely exchanged a few words—approached. Without preamble or platitudes, she sat next to me. She didn't try to downplay my mistake or offer quick fixes. She simply stayed there, quietly present. And in that moment, I understood something essential: authentic friendships don't emerge from how often you meet or message each other, but from the quality of the listening that can turn even a moment of discouragement into deeper understanding.

After that experience, I began to view my relationships through a different lens. No longer did I measure them by who appeared in party photos, but by who stayed close when the lights faded and success was nowhere to be found. A sincere friendship doesn't demand that you always shine; it won't flee at the sight of your tears. It's not based on mutual convenience or hollow flattery. On the contrary, those who truly care about you aren't afraid of your fragile side. In fact, it's during those vulnerable times that they reveal their true nature.

Think about the people you know: whom do you turn to when you trip up? Who responds with patience instead of irritation? Who notices your mood and takes the time to understand, rather than changing the subject? When you share a dream or a goal, who checks back later to see how things are going, subtly reminding you that your journey isn't invisible, but worthy of attention? These are the signs that distinguish a strong connection from a superficial one.

Imagine what would happen if, instead of settling for lukewarm relationships, you surrounded yourself with people able to sense your inner world without judging it. You might feel less inclined to hide your weaknesses, free to admit a mistake without fearing ridicule. You might discover a new strength—one not rooted in isolation, but in being encouraged to try, reassured in moments of doubt, and supported even when you don't have all the answers.

In the end, genuine friendships are the ones that don't leap off the boat when storms arise, but stay aboard, right beside you, providing a more stable balance in life's rough waters. You don't have to appear flawless, or pretend to always know what to do. A true friend accepts the complexity of your journey, not because it's easy, but because they see value in you that goes beyond momentary successes or failures. It's in this acceptance that trust takes shape, and during challenging times that these bonds reveal their unbreakable nature.

**Surrounding Yourself with Positive Energy**

Think about how it feels to enter a bright, well-ventilated room filled with plants and thoughtfully chosen furnishings. The atmosphere changes, your breathing becomes easier, and there's a sense of possibility. Human relationships work in a similar way. Some people create the effect of a stuffy room where the air barely circulates and every word feels heavy. Others, by contrast, offer a soft glow, like an open window looking out on a quiet garden. Surrounding yourself with positive energy isn't about chasing artificial perfection, but learning to recognize who makes your inner life feel more inhabitable.

Imagine a concrete scenario: you've had a tough day and your spirits are low. Who do you reach out to for a conversation or a moment of relief? There's that one person who, without ignoring your difficulties, manages to remind you that you've overcome hard times before and that nothing is set in stone. It's not forced optimism, but an attitude that highlights your strengths. This person doesn't belittle your problems nor pretend they'll vanish on their own; instead, they guide the conversation toward solutions or at least a broader perspective.

Positive energy also plays a role over the long term. Being surrounded by individuals who appreciate your uniqueness, who laugh with you (not at you), and who listen to your ideas without mocking them, creates a mentally stimulating environment. It's not a luxury, but an essential ingredient for personal growth. Positive energy doesn't mean avoiding conflict, but approaching it with respect, searching for common ground rather than easy victories at someone else's expense.

Try a simple experiment: over the next few days, notice how you feel after spending time with different people. Write down two or three words describing your mood after each encounter or conversation. Do you feel lighter, motivated, curious? Or do you sense tension, irritation, or emptiness? This basic monitoring helps you distinguish who adds value to your life. It's not about labeling people as good or bad, but about recognizing which dynamics nourish you and which drain you.

Also consider that you, too, can contribute positively. Energy doesn't flow in just one direction. If you want a brighter environment, you could start by being the source of that light. This doesn't mean forcing a smile when you don't feel like it, but genuinely sharing appreciation, paying attention to others' qualities, and supporting someone who's learning something new. Offering comfort doesn't deplete you; it creates a virtuous cycle. Often, when we genuinely radiate positivity, we become a quiet reference point, inspiring those around us to do the same.

Surrounding yourself with positive energy also involves making brave choices. Sometimes you'll need to loosen ties that no longer contribute anything meaningful, to make room for relationships that, while not perfect, help you find better balance. There's no rush or rigidity in this process—only the desire to protect something precious: your emotional well-being. By choosing who you keep close, you create an inner space where you can breathe, grow, and flourish, knowing that every encounter can become a seed of renewed vitality.

## Dealing with Toxic Relationships

There comes a moment, while talking to someone you once trusted, when you feel a slight discomfort in your stomach. You're not entirely sure why—perhaps a half-whispered remark or a glance that seems to hide hostility. At first, you think you're overreacting, too sensitive. But over time, you notice a pattern: every time you share a small achievement, the other person downplays it or hints that it's nothing special. Every time you show a vulnerability, they take the opportunity to deliver a subtle jab. It's as if you're trying to grow a flower while he—or she—regularly snaps off the petals, all the while smiling.

The common reaction is to think, "Maybe I'm not strong enough, I need to learn to tolerate this." But constantly tolerating subtle contempt doesn't make you mature—it wears you out. Maturity isn't about enduring the impossible; it's about identifying the toxic core of a relationship and acting to protect yourself. It's a shift in perspective: instead of asking, "How can I please them more?" ask, "Why am I pouring energy into someone who seems to gain strength from belittling me?"

Toxic relationships are like contaminated soil: no matter how much you plant, your seedlings struggle to grow. This isn't about an occasional argument or a single tense moment. It's about a constant imbalance of power, where the other person subtly dominates you, makes you feel at fault, and sows doubts about your worth. Such an environment stifles personal growth, erodes self-esteem, and creates emotional dependency.

Try this exercise: for one week, note three instances when someone diminishes, criticizes, or mocks your ideas or feelings. Just record the facts and how you felt. At the end of the week, review what you've written. If recurring patterns emerge, it could indicate a toxic dynamic. Recognizing the problem is the first step—without awareness, you remain trapped in a cycle of making excuses.

How many times have you thought, "Maybe it's my fault, maybe I just don't know how to respond"? Perhaps it's the reflection of a limiting belief: the idea that you must be accepted at any cost. But what if you decided to protect your peace of mind? What if you set clear boundaries—no more conversations ending in subtle humiliation, no more guilt for saying "enough"? This doesn't mean being aggressive, but no longer offering yourself up as a target.

At this point, you might wonder, "But if I distance myself from this person, will I be alone?" It's a legitimate doubt. Still, a temporary solitude, fertile ground for healthier future relationships, is better than being entangled in a bond that erodes your self-esteem. Leaving contaminated soil creates space for planting new seeds—ones that someone more genuine can help you nurture.

Now that you're starting to recognize the signs, a question arises: will you have the courage to cross the threshold and free yourself from what poisons your emotional roots? The answer isn't immediate, but on this path of recognition and transformation, your awareness has already carried you one step beyond the doorway.

**Creating a Safe Space Among Peers**

Imagine a place where, upon entering, you immediately feel at ease. Maybe it's a quiet corner at home where you can read uninterrupted, or a cozy little café with familiar faces. Now picture recreating something similar within your group of friends or classmates—a space where no one fears expressing their ideas, where people truly listen, and where differences aren't reasons for exclusion but sources of enrichment.

Creating a safe space among peers doesn't mean living in a world free of conflict or opposing opinions. Instead, it means ensuring that when disagreements arise, they're addressed with respect, with each person trying to understand the other's point of view. Not everyone will be a great speaker or always have the perfect words at hand, but a trusting environment allows for progress: those who feel welcomed dare to speak up, and those who feel heard learn how to refine their communication skills.

Think about typical situations in which "cliques" form and only a few set the unspoken rules, forcing others to conform or remain on the sidelines. In a safe space, these rigid boundaries soften. A new classmate, someone shy or from another town, can share something about themselves without fearing ridicule. Likewise, people already in the group can discover that by getting to know others better, they learn to see beyond prejudices and stereotypes.

How do you create this safe space in practice? Start with small, everyday habits. For example, the next time you're discussing a difficult topic in class or a study group, set a simple rule: each person can speak for one uninterrupted minute, and listeners commit to not mocking them, but rather mentally noting what's being said. At the end of each speech, before commenting, try to acknowledge at least one valid point in the other person's perspective, even if you don't fully agree. This simple exercise trains you in active listening and helps you identify constructive elements in every viewpoint.

Another key element is fostering informal moments where people share interests unrelated to school or daily obligations. An afternoon dedicated to board games or a walk in the park may lead you to discover hidden talents, shared passions, or surprising musical tastes. In these relaxed settings, you realize that everyone contributes a unique fragment of their personality to the group. Put together, these fragments form a more varied and harmonious mosaic.

Creating a safe space isn't a project accomplished in a single day. It requires consistency, a desire to improve, and a willingness to reflect on your own reactions. It's not an abstract goal, but a journey composed of many small steps, each reinforcing the feeling of moving in a healthy direction. The end result is an environment where peers don't just coexist, but learn to grow together, supporting one another and seeing diversity not as an obstacle, but as a strength.

# Chapter 8:
## Setting Personal Boundaries

*"Daring to set boundaries is about having the courage to love ourselves, even when we risk disappointing others." – Brené Brown*

Imagine a familiar situation: you accept an invitation to an event you don't really care about. You say yes out of habit, to avoid misunderstandings or disapproving looks. You spend the afternoon wrestling with an uneasy feeling, like carrying an invisible weight in your stomach. Maybe you would have preferred to devote that time to a personal interest or simply enjoy a quiet moment. Instead, you're stuck in a situation that doesn't reflect your needs. By the end of the day, you feel tired—not so much because of the event itself, but because you ignored your inner needs. It's as if you've had to pay an emotional toll just to keep up a façade of constant availability.

This scenario isn't rare. You often take on requests that leave you dissatisfied. You agree out of conformity, fear of disappointing others, or the worry of appearing "overly sensitive." Yet there's another way. You can choose to protect your peace of mind, to sharpen the line between what you truly want and what the rest of the world expects of you. Setting clear boundaries doesn't mean building impenetrable walls; it's about outlining an inner space where you can recharge, a symbolic place where your balance isn't sacrificed on the altar of external pressures.

The idea of a "personal boundary" represents the dividing line between what you're willing to embrace and what you prefer to keep out. This includes unwanted commitments, pressure to conform to something that doesn't feel right, and requests that breed tension. Establishing a boundary isn't an act of shutting people out, but one of caring for yourself—a conscious choice that reflects respect and consideration for your inner space. This chapter will guide you in understanding the value of these limits, learning how to express them with clarity and confidence, and facing any negative reactions without succumbing to guilt. You'll discover that protecting your peace of mind is a habit you build step by step.

## Understanding the Value of Your Own Limits

Think of every boundary as a line drawn on the map of your life. It marks where invasive demands end and where your own quiet space begins. Recognizing the value of this line means giving yourself permission to listen to your deeper inclinations. Without a clear boundary, you risk spending your days trying to meet everyone else's expectations, silently accumulating frustration. On the other hand, defining what protects your psychological integrity helps create a more peaceful environment.

When you decide to treat your boundaries as precious elements, you recognize that you're under no obligation to please everyone. You don't have to say "yes" all the time just to feel accepted. In fact, the moment you grant yourself the right to choose how to manage your time and energy, you uncover unexpected inner resources. Every boundary you draw erases a bit of background noise, freeing up space for activities that nurture your mind, for genuinely stimulating relationships, for endeavors that resonate with your nature.

A well-defined boundary takes nothing away from your sensitivity. On the contrary, it allows you to safeguard it. If you used to believe that accepting any request was a sign of generosity, now you can think again. Being generous doesn't mean ignoring your needs. Rather, it means deciding under which conditions you're willing to share your presence. By setting a healthy limit, you affirm: "I have worth even if I don't meet every expectation." This act reduces the risk of ending up in unsatisfying situations, preserving your clarity and emotional well-being.

Consider that each time you acknowledge a personal boundary, you learn to weigh the different elements of your reality more fairly: requests, proposals, social obligations. It's not about raising barricades, but about carefully evaluating what deserves a place in your inner world. Focusing on what makes you feel good doesn't push others away. In fact, it brings you closer to more genuine relationships because you meet people without pretending their needs automatically outweigh your own. Embracing the value of boundaries means offering yourself a more mature perspective, a balanced understanding of relationships, and a new way of building authentic connections.

With every line you draw on your life's map, the landscape becomes clearer. Far from the chaos of a thousand overlapping voices, a peaceful space emerges where your identity can breathe with ease. Here, your mind no longer has to constantly defend itself from invisible intruders. With each recognized boundary, you learn to care for your inner dimension, protecting your peace of mind as a precious resource.

**Expressing Boundaries Clearly**

Think about those moments when you face a request that makes you uncomfortable. Maybe a last-minute invitation, or a favor that disrupts your plans. You might smile nervously, offer vague excuses, stall until the conversation fades without a concrete answer. In those moments, you feel a slight twinge of guilt, as if your silence implies wrongdoing. And yet, you have the option to use clear words, unmistakable signals, firmly drawing the line between what you truly want and what you see as a burden stealing space from your peace of mind.

To communicate a boundary, you need a decisive tone, steady eye contact, and brief, direct statements spoken naturally. Uncertainty breeds misunderstandings, confuses the listener, and feeds the notion that one can keep pressing without consequences. Expressing a limit doesn't require shouting, nor a list of countless reasons to justify your "no." A few well-chosen words, a pause that underscores your resolve, and the awareness that a clearly set boundary will ease future tension—that's all you need.

Picture speaking with a classmate who keeps pushing you to join an extracurricular project you're not interested in. You might say, "I appreciate your idea, but I'd rather focus on other things right now." Notice this example: few words, no vague promises, no unnecessary explanations. You're not blaming anyone, not belittling the other person's idea, not making excuses. You're simply stating a truth: you have other priorities. This style of communication respects you and doesn't negate your regard for the other person. You express a refusal without turning it into a confrontation.

Clarity thrives on simplicity. Avoid beating around the bush, since every extra detail invites objections. If you try to soften your refusal too much, you risk sounding uncertain. When your tone and content align, your words carry greater credibility. If your voice stays steady, your hands still, and your gaze meets the other person's, they receive a clear signal: your decision doesn't depend on their approval.

You can practice saying "no" on your own, imagining hypothetical scenarios. Preparing in advance reduces awkwardness. Saying concise phrases helps you internalize a natural defense mechanism, making the boundary part of who you are. So when the time comes to say it to someone in real life, you won't feel guilty, nor think you need to justify yourself. You'll know exactly how to say what you mean, avoiding a dance of excuses and half-truths.

Words become building blocks for a sturdy boundary. Each clear statement strengthens your sense of self-worth. You prove to yourself that your emotional integrity isn't for sale, that your voice deserves to be heard. The other person will understand the nature of your position. They might be surprised or disappointed, but that well-defined boundary will force them to respect your choice. Over time, those who deal with you will learn not to cross that line. Meanwhile, you'll gain more energy, more clarity, and more inner space to cultivate what truly matters to you.

## Handling Others' Negative Reactions

Imagine you've just drawn a boundary, even a small one. Perhaps you've politely declined an invitation, explained that you'd rather focus on something else at the moment, or finally put a stop to a continuous request for help that's been wearing you down. And here it comes: surprise, irritation, maybe disappointment. You notice the other person no longer smiles as naturally, their tone grows harsher, or they abruptly change the subject. You might feel unsettled, as though a sudden wave of tension has washed over your exchange. It's understandable: setting a limit can throw off someone who was used to seeing you always ready to comply.

The first thing to remember is that the other person's reaction isn't a problem you need to solve. If you look calmly, you'll realize you're doing nothing wrong by protecting your peace. Even if their gaze sharpens or their words turn sarcastic, you don't owe anyone an explanation or an effort to ease their discomfort. Your priority remains honoring what feels right for you. If in the past you felt compelled to please others just to quell their irritations, now you recognize the steep mental cost of that habit. You have no obligation to maintain harmony at all costs.

If you face words of disapproval, you don't need to respond with aggression. Keep your tone measured, reply with a few essential sentences, and avoid unnecessary explanations. Remember: you didn't set this boundary to argue, but to safeguard your space. The other person might try to make you feel guilty or hint that you're no longer as accommodating as before. When that happens, pause. Breathe. Recognize that their emotional reactions are not yours, and it's not your responsibility to handle them. Your role isn't to soothe everyone else's unhappiness; it's to protect your own integrity.

Perhaps the other person will persist or try to convince you that you're overreacting. This is when your boundary proves its strength. You don't have to reopen the door you just closed, or reconsider what you've already stated. If your gaze still holds the conviction that you've been honest, if your posture doesn't slip into gestures of apology, if there's no hint of doubt in your voice, they'll realize there's no room to break through your decision. Eventually, they'll understand that insisting does them no good.

It's possible that, after a moment of tension, the situation will rebalance itself. But you shouldn't aim for this outcome or hope for instant approval. Keep in mind that someone who's been refused might need time to adjust their expectations. If you expressed your limit with respect and firmness, you've done your part. You can accept that the other person might be annoyed without making it your burden. You might even find that, down the road, this individual learns to consider you more carefully—respecting your space, your voice, your individuality, and your personal rhythms. In any case, you've already gained something priceless: the certainty that you can move through the world without feeling forced to sacrifice your peace of mind just to satisfy others.

## Strengthening Your Personal Space

Imagine having a small inner garden—a place that belongs solely to you and that no one can enter without your permission. At first, it might feel sparse, with only a few trees and barely defined paths. Over time, each time you set a boundary it's as if you plant a new shrub, add a shady bench, or better outline the trails winding among the trees. Gradually, that once hazy and indistinct garden takes shape. Your personal space grows more vivid, greener, and more capable of offering you respite whenever you need it.

Think of these boundaries as practical tools for enriching your inner life. Each time you respond firmly, each time you resist the temptation to yield just to keep the peace, you strengthen the roots in this space. Your mind learns to recognize what sustains you and what weakens you. As you get used to protecting your limits, you'll find yourself more quickly identifying signs of intrusion. There's no longer a lengthy debate in your mind about what troubles you—you sense it almost immediately. That's one sign of well-tended ground, where the plants flourish more luxuriantly.

The energy you gain from this heightened awareness isn't confined to your private haven. It reflects onto every area of your life: your studies, your relationships, your passions, your everyday choices. Like sunlight filtering through leafy branches, your renewed solidity brightens decisions that once felt murky. You begin to realize that always going along with others' requests robbed you of time to nurture your own interests. Now you have fertile soil to sow what you wish to learn, create, and experience.

This balance doesn't emerge by chance. It requires practice, consistency, and trust in your own feelings. Day after day, you can make small moves to reinforce your personal space: calmly saying "no" when a request doesn't align with you, closing your door for a few minutes of silence, defining times when you won't respond to messages so you can rest. It's not about erecting impenetrable walls, but about marking out pleasant, safe pathways where you can walk without the fear of unwanted bumps and shoves.

Over time, you'll notice that defending your boundaries isn't selfish. It means respecting your own priorities and recognizing that your desires deserve attention and space. Free of tension in your inner garden, you can approach others with greater sincerity, no longer pretending infinite availability. You find a balance between opening yourself to the world and safeguarding your essential core. Like a gardener who knows each plant by heart, you learn where to invest your energy and where careful containment is needed.

This work of inner cultivation, while not guaranteeing a life without challenges, brings a sense of greater solidity. Strolling through your garden, you feel the presence of deep roots and well-defined paths. In this personal space, which you've learned to protect with clear, decisive actions, you rediscover the strength of a serenity no longer threatened by external pressures. And that serenity, patiently nurtured, ultimately spreads into every corner of your life.

# A Small Gesture, A Big Impact

Have you ever thought about how powerful a simple gesture can be? Sometimes, it takes very little to make a big difference in someone else's life.

If this book has helped you understand yourself better, feel more confident, or see things from a new perspective, you have the opportunity to do something just as meaningful for another girl who's searching for answers.

By leaving a review, you can share your experience and guide others toward a similar journey. It doesn't have to be long or perfect—your honest perspective is what matters most. With just a few words, you can help someone who feels lost find the courage to start their own path of growth.

Your review might be the spark that lights up a new awareness in another young woman. It could be the bridge between her present and the better future she's looking for.

Thank you from the bottom of my heart for taking the time to make this gesture. Together, we can make a real difference in someone's life.

Scan to leave a review on Amazon if you live in the US

Scan to leave a review on Amazon if you live in the UK

Scan to leave a review on Amazon if you live in Canada

Scan to leave a review on Amazon if you live in Australia

# Chapter 9:
# Mastering Everyday Stress and Anxiety

*"You can't stop the waves, but you can learn to surf." – Jon Kabat-Zinn*

Imagine waiting your turn for a particularly challenging oral exam. The classroom is quiet, yet it feels as if you can hear a constant rustling, a rapid rhythm that keeps pace with your heartbeat. You sense the air heating up around you, your mouth going dry, your thoughts racing past like blurred images. The teacher calls your name: in that single moment, you experience the essence of a familiar inner state—stress. But what is this stress, really, that hits us unexpectedly? Why can a simple school situation trigger such an intense reaction?

The truth is, stress isn't just an invisible enemy; it's also a signal, a messenger trying to draw your attention to something. And anxiety, its traveling companion, isn't always a curse. Sometimes it's a bright warning light indicating the need to reorganize your resources and find balance. This chapter aims to provide tools for observing these states through a new lens, rather than succumbing to the idea that you're at the mercy of uncontrollable forces.

The goal? To understand how stress works, to identify the dynamics that generate it, and to recognize that behind discomfort there can be an opportunity. You'll discover practical strategies for taming tension, training your mind to transform anxiety into more manageable energy. You'll also learn how to build an inner refuge—a mental space you can return to when external pressures mount. The idea isn't to eliminate stress from your life—that would be unrealistic—but to make it less invasive, a force you can channel instead of endure. In the end, learning to "surf the waves" is a valuable skill: it doesn't deny the existence of the waves, but keeps you from being swept away.

## Unmasking the Mechanics of Stress

First, take a closer look. Examine the situations that unsettle you: an oral exam, a sports competition, an unexpected change to your daily plans. If you think about it, it's not the event itself that casts a shadow over your peace of mind. What triggers tension is how you interpret what's happening. The exam, for instance, isn't just a test; it becomes a measure of your personal worth. The shift in plans isn't just a small inconvenience; it's a threat to order and predictability. Your body and mind react to these internal narratives, not simply to the external facts.

The trick is to realize that your mind is constantly processing signals. Facing a challenge, your brain sets off an alarm, warning you of potential dangers and urging you to mobilize energy. So far, nothing unusual. In fact, this reaction has ancient roots, once priming you to fight or flee. But if you constantly perceive situations as threats, even when they aren't, your system remains tense, never allowing you to truly rest.

To unmask the mechanics of stress, try an exercise in awareness. Next time you feel nervous—sweaty palms, rapid breathing, racing thoughts—ask yourself: "What story am I telling myself?" Maybe you believe you're not good enough, or that one mistake will ruin others' respect for you. These interpretations act like distorting lenses: they magnify risks and minimize your strengths. By identifying them, you take the first step in rethinking your internal narrative.

Consider stress as a relationship between the demands of your environment and how you perceive your abilities. If you feel you lack the tools to face a situation, pressure rises. But what happens if you shift your perspective? If you admit that you can learn from the experience, prepare gradually, or ask for help, the sense of threat decreases. You haven't changed the external reality, only your point of view. And that's key: recognizing that stress takes root in your mind. Uprooting it doesn't mean removing every stimulus, but reducing their power over you.

Unmasking the mechanics of stress means moving from seeing it as an implacable enemy to viewing it as a message to decode. Each time stress appears, it tells you that something in your mental map has veered off course: exaggerated fears, rigid expectations, crushing comparisons. Learning to interpret this message—to distinguish facts from interpretations—gives your mind the freedom to choose how to react. In this freedom lies the chance to transform anxiety into a useful signal and stress into an ally that pushes you to better understand yourself.

## Strategies to Regain Your Calm

A silent pendulum sways, each swing marking a pace unlike the frenzy of your thoughts. Anxiety doesn't vanish in an instant; it grows gentler when given room to slow down. It's not about suppressing every emotion, but about guiding the mind beyond the storm, toward a spot where agitation loses its edge, like an echo fading into emptiness.

Among the most accessible techniques, mindful breathing holds a special place. When your heart speeds up and ideas tangle, no grand gestures are required. Focusing on your breath—the cool air flowing in, the warm air flowing out, the gentle rise and fall of your chest— provides an anchor in the simple repetition of a vital act. In just a few moments, muscles relax, your pulse settles into a calmer rhythm, and your mind recovers some of its autonomy.

Introducing brief intervals of quiet into your day can also make a difference. You don't need a full hour of meditation: even five minutes of total silence—perhaps sitting near a window, watching leaves dancing on the branches—or a short walk around the block, letting your ears tune into previously unnoticed background sounds, can help. These micro-breaks act like cushions between stressful events, stopping anxiety from piling up layer by layer.

Sometimes small gestures of self-care help reclaim serenity. Gently massaging your hands with a pleasantly scented cream, stroking a pet's soft fur, slowly sipping a warm herbal tea—each of these moments creates a kinder sensory microcosm. Touch, smell, taste— these senses step forward, cutting through mental overload and grounding you in the here and now.

Another option involves recalling a reassuring scene: a hilltop path, a sunlit clearing, or the coziest room in your home. Walking through these details in your mind, envisioning colors and distant sounds, helps lower the internal volume. The problem doesn't disappear, but your gaze shifts to a different vantage point. What once seemed like an unscalable wall now feels more like a challenge with greater perspective.

Choosing the most effective method is personal. Some find relief by writing their worries onto a blank page, others prefer movement— perhaps dancing quietly in their room or doing a few stretches. Over time, you build an "emotional first-aid kit" from which you can draw, depending on the situation. Little by little, what once seemed insurmountable becomes more manageable. The secret isn't to deny discomfort, but to develop tools for traversing it without being swept away, floating above the surface of anxiety, one mindful breath at a time.

**Turning Anxiety into Concrete Action**

Certain feelings arrive like quiet signals. Anxiety, in these moments, doesn't show up to complicate your life but rather to point toward possible directions. A knot in your stomach, tense shoulders, racing thoughts—these are useful indicators, not only of what troubles you but also of the steps you need to take to find a more solid way forward.

To begin, break your goal down into smaller parts. If a school test makes you nervous, tackling it one chapter at a time can make the workload more manageable. Similarly, if the thought of a tough conversation paralyzes you, decide on the first sentence you'll say. Each fragment of action marks a small victory, eases the tension, and transforms nebulous unease into precise movements.

Creating a concrete plan reduces uncertainty. Writing out a sequence of tasks, preparing your materials in advance, and setting realistic time frames for each phase all help turn anxiety from an abstract presence into a driving force. Your thoughts no longer drift in fear of the unknown; they anchor themselves to a plan, a guide that shapes your every step. Seen this way, anxiety becomes an alert, not an intimidation—encouraging you to stay focused.

There's tremendous power in choosing to gather information and seek support. Anxiety can prompt you to consult someone who knows the subject well, to skim a concise guide on a complex topic, or to talk it over with a more experienced classmate. Every question asked, every source checked, every opinion heard transforms tension into a means of filling gaps and gaining confidence. Uncertainty loses some of its influence when you shrink the space it needs to grow.

Setting clear objectives is a crucial milestone. Without a goal, anxiety hovers in a vague, undefined state. But by identifying a concrete target, all that excess energy finds the right direction. It pushes you to practice more, to get organized, to stop procrastinating. With a clearly defined purpose, these physical sensations are no longer pointless: they encourage more deliberate actions, giving meaning to your initial unease.

The idea of experimenting with alternatives also takes on new significance. If you're afraid you're not ready for a presentation, try

73

rehearsing in front of a mirror or record yourself so you can listen back with some distance. These concrete actions turn anxiety into a reason to improve your performance. You're no longer fighting an invisible monster; instead, you're sharpening your tools, making better use of the resources you have.

As you move into action, anxiety shrinks to a more manageable size. It doesn't disappear, but it no longer rules the scene. Instead, it becomes a traveling companion that urges you to be more organized, more aware of your abilities, and more ready to step in when necessary. In this view, anxiety emerges as a catalyst for effective action: it doesn't weigh you down; it offers you the opportunity to develop more adaptive, concrete responses.

## Creating an Inner Refuge of Serenity

Think of a cherished object you always carry with you—maybe a pendant, a photo, or simply a pen that inspires calm. Its physical presence may be small, but the symbolic value it holds can open a doorway in your mind. In a similar way, building an inner refuge means creating a mental space you can retreat to when the outside world presses in and tensions threaten to overwhelm. There's no need for physical walls or keys to enter; your ability to focus your attention on elements that bring tranquility grants you access.

To start, choose a reassuring memory. Maybe it's a sunny afternoon spent chatting with a friend, the sound of a song you listened to during a happy time, or the gentle light of a room that welcomed you after a tiring day. Just one fragment—a feeling, an image, a scent— will do. Bring it to mind, examine its details calmly, "listen" to the sensations it evokes. By doing so, you mark a path toward a protected place where no outside criticism and no looming deadline can unbalance you.

An inner refuge of serenity works like an anchor. When anxiety whispers that you don't have enough time, that you're not good enough, that everything is slipping out of your grasp, you can return here. It doesn't take much—maybe a minute or two of pause. Close your eyes and summon that memory, that image. Notice how the grip of unease loosens. The world hasn't disappeared, your problems haven't magically dissolved, yet now you have a broader perspective, a state of mind less at the mercy of fears.

This refuge isn't a luxury to indulge in sparingly, but a tool you can call on whenever you need it. With practice, entering it becomes easier, almost like recalling the title of a favorite book. The more you use it, the more solid its mental structure becomes, the richer the details. Start with a single element—a face, a sound, a color. Then add more pieces until you've drawn a small map of peace.

To enhance the effect, you can pair this visualization with a physical gesture, such as holding a smooth stone or interlacing your fingers. A simple, repeatable action sends a signal to your body and mind that it's time to seek shelter in that private corner. Your inner refuge doesn't replace reality or deny the challenges you face. It simply offers a foothold, a steady point from which to move forward again.

Over time, this practice trains your mind not to be trapped in anxiety's spirals. It's like having a second compass, an internal reference that reminds you that no matter how frantic the world around you, there's a calm, secure space deep inside you. A place that doesn't depend on external validation, flawless results, or others' opinions, but solely on your ability to direct your attention toward what brings you serenity. A place where you can catch your breath, gather your thoughts, and return to reality with greater stability.

# Chapter 10:
# Rediscovering Strength in Failure

*"Failure is simply the opportunity to begin again, this time more intelligently." – Henry Ford*

There's a particular feeling that takes shape when the result you aimed for crumbles before your eyes. Maybe it was an exam you prepared for meticulously, an audition you felt you could ace, or a sports competition you were sure you could win. After all your effort, you're left staring at an unsatisfactory score, a rejection, a dream slipping away. In that moment, a sort of emptiness settles inside you: you might feel inadequate, disoriented, as if your very identity has taken a hit.

But is it really like that? Does a failure capture your worth forever, or is it just a fragment of a bigger journey you're still writing? If you look at the stories of people you admire, you'll notice a common pattern: behind every great success lies a series of obstacles overcome, moments of falling and rising again. The difference lies in how you interpret the mistake. Those who see it as proof of their incompetence risk getting stuck. Those who accept it as a signal—an inevitable phase of the growth process—gain a new lens through which to view events.

This chapter aims to help you reimagine failure, no longer as the ultimate judge of your abilities, but as an opportunity for understanding, adjustment, and growth. The goal is not to encourage carelessness or downplay the disappointment of an unmet goal. Rather, it's to offer tools for recalibrating the meaning of mistakes and transforming them into a driving force for more conscious progress.

## Recalibrating the Meaning of Mistakes

The word "failure" has a harsh, definitive sound. It evokes the image of a door slamming shut, sealing off the room where you placed your hopes. But what if we change perspective? Consider the possibility that every error isn't a verdict on your personal worth, but an indicator. An indicator of what, exactly? Of where you can intervene, which skills need refining, which strategies need rethinking.

When a goal goes unmet, the instinctive reaction might be to pull back, to avoid new challenges for fear of experiencing the same frustration. However, this approach doesn't ease the pain; it preserves it like a snapshot. A different interpretation of mistakes can set a far more productive process in motion. Think about it: every time you fail, you're gathering valuable information. You're discovering which approaches are less effective, which factors you overlooked, and what kind of preparation might strengthen your future efforts.

In other words, an error becomes a diagnostic tool, not a permanent mark of failure. Recognizing this means accepting imperfection as an integral part of the journey. No one moves forward in a perfectly straight line. Even the most successful people you see shining in their fields have collected a series of attempts that went wrong. They didn't label themselves as incapable; they used those experiences to fine-tune their skills, improve their organization, and create more effective methods.

Recalibrating the meaning of mistakes, then, requires a change in mindset. Instead of telling yourself, "I failed, I'm not good enough," you could say, "This attempt didn't yield the desired results, now I know better where to make adjustments." It's a shift that takes courage, because it means leaving behind a rigid view where you're either a winner or a loser, and embracing a more nuanced one where failure is just another event—one that serves a specific purpose: highlighting where you can grow.

This change in perspective doesn't erase disappointment. The bitterness may still be there, and it deserves to be acknowledged. Yet you don't let it dictate your self-worth. The error isn't a judgment on your identity but a pointer that shows you which areas need more light. By adopting this view, failure loses some of its crushing weight, making room for constructive reflection. It's like moving from staring at a crack in the wall and despairing, to seeing that same crack as an opportunity to understand where the structure needs reinforcement. In this way, mistakes become part of the journey, not the final destination.

## Drawing Lessons from Setbacks

Picture a craftsman at work: they run their hand over the wood, feel its imperfections, discard an initial idea if it's not working, add a new piece, smooth an edge. Every flaw, every crack, offers a clue for improving the final shape. In a similar way, the setbacks you encounter along your path aren't just unlucky detours to forget about. You can turn them into genuine "maps" to guide you more effectively.

A practical way to extract lessons is to calmly analyze the situation, much like a researcher confronting a failed experiment. Instead of simply saying, "I failed," ask yourself: What factors led me to this outcome? Was there a lack of preparation? Did you underestimate the time needed? Did you rely on unsuitable strategies? Focusing on the elements contributing to the disappointing result lets you identify critical issues, like a mechanic listening to engine noises to figure out where to fix things.

This exercise requires honesty. You might notice that sometimes your eagerness to shine right away stifled caution, or that the fear of judgment kept you from asking for help in time. What you discover shouldn't be used as a weapon against yourself, but as a resource for the future. Identifying mistakes doesn't mean beating yourself up; it means knowing which keys to press next time. Nobody expects a perfect solution on the first try: the art of improvement involves constant adjustments.

Another approach involves breaking down the failure into stages. Imagine drawing a timeline: one end shows the initial goal, the other the actual outcome. Mark the key moments along the way—your preparation, the decisions made, moments of doubt, the unexpected twist. Reviewing them in this linear perspective allows you to place every event in context, avoiding the trap of fixating on the final step alone. Often, failure arises from a series of small choices rather than one glaring, monumental error. Identifying the pattern that led to the slip-up makes it easier to correct your course.

The ability to draw lessons from setbacks isn't limited to the present. Over time, you'll accumulate a repertoire of practical lessons—a kind of internal library. Each past failure becomes a reference point: "That time I acted too quickly and it didn't work out; now I know I need more time." Or: "I ignored the advice of someone more experienced, and next time I'll pay closer attention." This archive of accumulated experience will make you more flexible, more prepared to adapt to new challenges, and less likely to be frightened by an unexpected obstacle.

Cultivating a curious mindset is key. Instead of retreating into disappointment, consider failure as a messenger delivering useful information. You might even find hints for alternative paths, solutions you never considered, or a new route you'd never have explored without that stumble. In this way, a mistake isn't just a dark moment, but a springboard from which you can leap toward more mature approaches, bolder ideas, and more solid plans. Every defeat, when examined with openness, becomes a pencil you can use to redraw the outlines of your journey.

## Strengthening Your Inner Resilience

Imagine resilience as an invisible muscle, hidden beneath the surface of your certainties. Each stumble, each mistake, each outcome that falls short of your expectations works like silent training, shaping your ability to bounce back. Unlike a physical muscle, resilience doesn't develop through weights and barbells, but through the mindset you bring to facing difficulties.

A first step in strengthening it is letting go of the idea that life should follow a straight line. Instead of being surprised when things don't go as planned, accept that veering off course isn't an exception, but a part of the journey itself. This awareness reduces the shock of failure: if you expect some turbulence, you won't be knocked down by it. The secret isn't to avoid obstacles, but to handle them when they arise.

Another crucial element is learning to tolerate uncertainty. Often, the fear of making mistakes stems from the belief that you must control every aspect. But reality is more nuanced. You might not be able to manage all factors, yet you can control how you respond to what happens. Embracing a degree of unpredictability and doing your best even in less-than-ideal situations is an excellent way to grow your resilience. The more you train your mind to navigate a sea of variables, the less you'll fear not having everything under control.

There's also power in being kind to yourself. After a setback, you might be tempted to scold yourself harshly, listing all your shortcomings. But resilience thrives on compassion. Speak to yourself as you would to a friend: instead of focusing solely on the failure, acknowledge the effort, dedication, and courage it took to try. This perspective doesn't let you off the hook for your mistakes—it simply helps you avoid confusing the outcome of an attempt with your value as a person.

The ability to seek help when needed also strengthens resilience. Often, the sense of defeat intensifies if you shut yourself off, avoiding any discussion out of fear of judgment. Reaching out to a friend, a family member, a teacher, or a mentor can offer new perspectives and advice. Sharing the burden lightens the pressure and shows that you're not alone on your path to growth. It's an exchange of energy that turns vulnerability into a bridge toward stronger solutions.

Over time, each time you overcome a small or large difficulty, you add a brick to the foundation of your resilience. You become more flexible, ready to regain balance after a jolt. This doesn't mean you stop feeling pain or frustration; it means you can incorporate them into your personal story without letting them define you. A failure then becomes one ingredient in the overall recipe, not the only flavor on your plate. It increases your ability to see beyond the present moment, recognizing that while the road to your goals may have steep climbs, you'll grow steadily stronger along the way.

**Building a Growth-Oriented Mindset**

Imagine viewing your experiences through the eyes of an explorer, rather than a harsh judge. A mistake stops being a permanent stain and becomes a sign pointing toward new territories to discover. This idea is linked to the concept of a "growth mindset," where abilities and skills aren't static entities, but qualities that can be cultivated through effort, flexibility, and continuous learning.

Embracing a growth-oriented mindset means not assuming that if you struggled with something today, it will always be that way. Instead, it means viewing failure as a temporary condition, not an irreversible fate. Someone who adopts this approach doesn't ask, "Why am I not good at this?" but rather, "How can I improve?" The focus shifts from seeing a fixed limitation to seeking strategies that expand your capabilities.

One helpful step is to stop constantly comparing yourself to others. Instead of looking enviously at those who seem to excel effortlessly, concentrate on your own personal trajectory. Every small improvement becomes a milestone: learning a new study technique, finding a creative solution to a problem, refining your skills in a sport or an art form. Growth doesn't require an instant leap to perfection, but gradual steps that, over time, build a solid foundation.

Often, adopting a growth mindset also involves giving new meaning to negative feedback. Rather than interpreting it as a judgment of your worth, consider it as a suggestion on where to direct your efforts. A teacher pointing out an error in your assignment isn't saying you're incapable, but highlighting an area to work on. The same goes for a friend or family member who notices a shortcoming. Instead of feeling attacked, you can ask yourself what you can learn from their observation.

This doesn't mean accepting every comment uncritically, but knowing how to distinguish between constructive criticism and mere attacks. A growth mindset helps you filter the input you receive from the outside world: take what's useful, discard what isn't. This makes you more independent in your journey, less likely to be swayed by others' opinions, and better able to incorporate valuable insights into your evolution.

Over time, this perspective changes the way you relate to failure. You no longer fear it as an enemy to run from, but see it as an uncomfortable yet valuable ally, teaching you and honing your skills. Growing doesn't mean avoiding mistakes, but using them as stepping stones. Each time you fall, you rise up a bit stronger, a bit more aware, a bit more confident in your potential. Ultimately, a growth-oriented mindset transforms your landscape: no longer a horizon blocked by insurmountable limits, but a wide, varied space where you can move forward with curiosity and determination.

# Chapter 11:
# Exploring Hidden Passions and Talents

*"Your passion is waiting for your courage to catch up." – Isabelle Laflèche*

Do you remember the first time you tried playing an instrument just by instinct, without a single lesson under your belt? Maybe it was a worn-out guitar forgotten in the attic, or an old flute you found in your mother's desk drawer. Back then, you probably weren't thinking, "I'm discovering a talent." And yet something clicked. That sense of novelty, that keen curiosity, was a clue: there are parts of you still unexplored. It's a bit like moving a piece of old furniture in your living room and suddenly noticing a corner of the room you never saw before.

The truth is, our abilities often hide behind the everyday: routines, habits, external expectations. We follow the same path because it's familiar, never venturing beyond the well-trodden trail. And so we end up asking ourselves: "What if I'm good at something I've never tried?" That question carries a subtle power, opening the door to unexpected possibilities, unexplored perspectives, scenarios waiting to be unveiled. This chapter aims to help you welcome that question with courage, to transform curiosity into action and uncertainty into discovery. In the pages ahead, you'll learn how to identify your aptitudes, give yourself permission to try new avenues, and broaden your horizons.

Picture a journey of transformation: at first, you feel confined to a fixed role, unable to see alternatives; along the way, you decide to give yourself the chance to explore without judgment; and in the end, you're surprised to find hidden resources and strengths that expand your vision. The goal isn't to instantly become "the best" at something, but to embark on a path of continuous learning. Even a small step can widen your perspective. Every new activity you try, every creative gesture you experiment with, is like opening a window onto your potential.

## Identifying Your Aptitudes

Think back to a day in your childhood when you got completely lost in doing something without even realizing it. Maybe you spent hours drawing, immersed in creating worlds of color; or made up stories in your head while walking home alone; or solved little puzzles, fixing broken objects with naive patience. Those moments weren't just passing diversions, but clues to what comes naturally to you—what your mind and heart do effortlessly, almost playfully.

Identifying your aptitudes means stepping back and observing your behavior without judgment. Ask yourself: "What activities make me lose track of time?" "What energizes me instead of draining me?" "Which situations make me feel alive, curious, fulfilled?" Don't just think about what's "useful" or "profitable." Focus on what resonates with your essence. Sometimes, aptitudes emerge in unexpected contexts: cooking for friends, improvising a dance when no one's watching, spending an afternoon studying constellations from your balcony.

It helps to experiment without the obsession of having to excel right away. If you try writing a short story and find that the words flow easily, you might have stumbled onto a narrative streak you didn't know you had. If you pick up a new musical instrument and discover your fingers learn quickly, or if you take photos and find yourself thrilled by the way light filters through the leaves, these feelings are valuable signals. The key is to learn how to recognize the messages your own behavior sends you.

Talking to people who know you well can also help. Ask a friend, "When do you see me really engaged?" Sometimes others notice inclinations you take for granted. An outside observer can provide a "mirror," revealing talents you consider normal but are actually unique. Perhaps you think everyone's good at listening with empathy, while those around you see your capacity for understanding others as something truly special.

**Trying Out New Interests**

Imagine walking along a forest path, dappled light filtering through the trees, reflecting on a shiny stone and catching your attention. You crouch down, pick it up, examine it closely: you have no idea if it's valuable, but it piques your curiosity, making you wonder where it might lead. Exploring new interests is a bit like picking up that stone: you don't know if it will bring you anything useful, but the simple act of bending down for a closer look opens up possibilities you hadn't considered before.

Think about it: how many times have you told yourself, "That's not for me," without ever really giving it a shot? Maybe you dismissed the idea of taking a theater class, afraid you'd feel out of place. Or you gave up on learning a foreign language because you didn't think you were "cut out" for it. But what if you flipped the starting point? Instead of asking if you're talented at something, you might ask, "How do I feel while I'm doing this?" It's like discovering a new ingredient in cooking: you won't know if you like it until you taste it.

You can start with simple activities, without committing a lot of time or money. Look up online tutorials and try making something small with your own hands, attend a trial session of a contemporary dance class, or read a book about a topic you know nothing about. The key is allowing yourself the luxury of being a beginner, of not having immediate answers. We often hesitate because we're afraid we won't be good at something right away, forgetting that skill isn't a prerequisite—it's something you develop over time.

When you approach something new, you're also training your adaptability. Whether it's a new sport, a craft hobby, or a musical instrument, it doesn't matter: facing the unknown teaches you to handle uncertainty. And if you discover it's not for you, it's not a failure—just another piece of your personal experience puzzle. Every interest you set aside helps you better define the path you want to follow, like a navigation system adjusting your route.

In the end, exploring new interests is like opening windows onto different mental landscapes. Even if you end up closing a window because you don't love the view, you've still learned something: maybe you noticed a previously overlooked detail, understood a new aspect of yourself, or practiced patience. As you gather these fragments of experience, you become more flexible, more inclined to say, "Why not?" and gradually expand your definition of who you are.

## Turning Hobbies into Sources of Fulfillment

Have you ever spent an entire afternoon doing something simply because it interested you, with no reason other than your own curiosity? Consider my friend Marta, for example. During a stressful period at work, she took out an old box of oil pastels. She hadn't touched art materials in years, yet this time she sat on the floor and began drawing lines on white sheets of paper, without expectations, without striving for impressive results. At first, she felt unsure, as if she were peeking into someone else's world. But after a few minutes, the gentle rustle of the paper, the softness of the color, the slightly earthy scent of the pigments created a different atmosphere—warm and reassuring. In that quiet world of color, Marta realized she was feeling a subtle calm, a small joy that depended on no one's approval but her own.

The truth is, a hobby can become a refuge—a protected corner where the rush and pressure of daily life stay outside. There's no need to show it to anyone, no need to prove anything. If you like strumming a few chords on your guitar as evening falls, or embroidering a small pattern on fabric, you do it because your mind finds a different rhythm: slower, more relaxed. In that repeated gesture, in listening to that imperfect melody, there's a sense of freedom where judgment drifts away.

You don't have to be good at it. With practice, sure, you'll improve, but even if you don't, it doesn't matter. The satisfaction comes from the process itself, from letting your creative energy flow without any particular goal. This mindset also changes how you approach other challenges in life. If, for example, you gradually learn how to knead bread or recognize aromatic herbs in a garden, you realize that learning isn't always tied to practical targets—it can also be fueled by curiosity and the pleasure of discovery.

In the end, that hobby—perhaps born from a vague desire or a timid attempt—becomes a small wellspring of well-being. Each practice session offers a moment of pause where you don't have to rush, don't have to compete, don't have to answer to anyone. And when you return to your daily tasks, you feel as if you've breathed lighter air, as if you've reconnected with yourself in a way that would otherwise remain buried under obligations. It's not about escaping, but about granting yourself a genuine space where you can simply be.

**Defining Your Own Unique Path**

Imagine standing at a fork in the road: one trail leads to a bright, open meadow; the other winds through dense, silent trees. Both can offer interesting landscapes, and both may hide unexpected challenges. The choice is yours, and there is no universal map telling you which direction is the "right" one. The same goes for discovering your talents: there isn't a single path that suits everyone, but rather a range of possibilities that can take shape based on your inclinations, interests, and pace.

Defining your own unique path means recognizing that you're not obligated to follow anyone else's footsteps. You might have seen a friend turn their love for handcrafted jewelry into a small online store, or a classmate devote themselves to a sport until they achieved competitive results. Such scenarios can inspire you, but you don't have to feel bound to replicate their goals or strategies. Each person is a blend of experiences, emotions, and curiosities, and this blend shapes a journey that's one-of-a-kind.

Ask yourself: "What would I truly enjoy doing if there were no rankings, grades, or judgments from others?" Maybe you want to dive deeper into a hobby with no intention of profit, just to see where it takes you. Or perhaps you'd like to weave a hidden passion into what you already do, creating a richer, more varied balance in your life. The beauty of your path lies in its openness: you don't need to define it all today. You can move forward step by step, observing how you respond to experiences and adjusting your trajectory as you go.

When you allow yourself to follow your passions—even the less conventional ones—you often discover unexpected connections. Maybe your love for cooking finds common ground with your knack for writing, inspiring you to create a recipe blog infused with storytelling. Or your curiosity about botany intertwines with your photography skills, prompting you to explore natural landscapes and document them with fresh sensitivity. In this dance of interests, you're no longer limited to single roles. Instead, you can mix elements to create something unique that truly reflects your identity.

Defining your path doesn't mean entering a final destination into life's GPS, but rather learning how to navigate using the signs you encounter along the way. It's a process of listening, in which you learn to distinguish what nourishes you from what leaves you empty, what helps you grow from what holds you back. This way, each stage becomes an opportunity for reflection: does this new interest deserve more space? Can this emerging talent connect to other aspects of my life?

In the end, there is no ultimate finish line, only a continuous movement. Learning to define your own unique path means gaining the freedom to move boundaries, change direction, experiment, and, if necessary, backtrack to try another route. It's a journey where what matters isn't coming in first, but exploring honestly who you are and what shapes your potential can take.

# Chapter 12:
# Mindfulness Rituals and Self-Care

*"The present moment is filled with joy and happiness. If you are attentive, you will see it." – Thich Nhat Hanh*

One evening, after a never-ending day of studying and chores, I found myself sitting in a chair, staring into empty space. Outside the window, the gentle hush of the street; inside, the warm glow of a desk lamp. It was quiet all around, yet my mind was in a state of restless commotion. I felt as though I had been running for hours without ever leaving the room. I closed my eyes, took a deep breath, and let my shoulders relax. That simple act—stopping, feeling my breath, allowing my thoughts to settle on something steadier—was like loosening a tight knot in my chest. In that moment, I realized I didn't have to wait for some vacation or special event to find a bit of calm: I could create my own small rituals to realign my inner balance, even on the busiest days.

This idea, the possibility of cultivating moments of mindful presence, doesn't require big tools or endless time. No special equipment, no exclusive setting is needed. A single minute is enough to turn your attention to your heartbeat, to the feeling of your feet on the floor, to the temperature of the air on your skin. Through mindfulness rituals and acts of self-care, you can learn to recognize the signals your body and mind send you, gently bringing your focus back to the here and now. Over time, this practice becomes a precious ally for easing tension, lightening the load of stress, and bringing forth a more authentic sense of serenity.

## Discovering the Joy of Presence

Think back to one of your most hectic afternoons: maybe juggling classes, endless messages to answer, and a pile of tasks that seemed never-ending. In that whirlwind, it's easy not to notice where you are, how you're breathing, or what expression you're wearing on your face. It's as if your mind is wandering elsewhere, jumping from one thought to another. That's where a small ritual comes in: pause for just a moment and draw your attention to something simple, present, and real.

You don't need to do anything complicated. Even placing one hand on your chest and feeling the rhythm of your breath might be enough. You'll notice that by slowing down the flow of thoughts and focusing on a single point, the rest of the world doesn't disappear—it just becomes a bit less intrusive. It's like giving your mind a quiet corner where it can reorganize its ideas without the pressure of having to run in all directions at once.

Gradually, these moments of awareness become small anchors to hold onto when your inner world feels turbulent. It's a bit like being in a crowded room and suddenly spotting a friendly face: you relax, relieved by the reassuring presence. In the same way, your conscious attention becomes a steady point you can rely on to regain calm when everything seems to be in upheaval.

## Creating Moments of Restorative Pause

Imagine a day when every task seems to slot into the next, like the pieces of an overly crowded mosaic. You wake up early, check your phone, answer some messages, head off to school, study, maybe attend an afternoon activity, then go home, tidy your room, prepare dinner, and dive into another study session. By the end of the evening, you feel as though you've just run an obstacle course without ever slowing down. In this endless flow of actions and thoughts, you might never have found a true moment to stop, to let your mind and body settle back into place.

Yet it only takes a few minutes to carve out a small island of calm—a restorative pause that doesn't demand major effort. This isn't just about taking a deep breath (you already know how to do that), but about introducing slightly different gestures or experiences. For example, try a "sensory pause": wherever you are, focus on a single sense. If you're in the school hallway, place a hand on the wall and notice its temperature, its texture. If you're at your desk, pick up an object with an interesting surface and study its details calmly. This simple act of sensory focus pulls you back into the present, quieting mental noise.

Or choose a symbolic gesture. Close your eyes for a moment and imagine setting down an invisible weight: a package that contains all the small anxieties accumulated so far. Picture yourself gently placing it by a wall, knowing that when you get moving again, you won't have to carry it along. Even just this metaphor can create a sense of lightness.

If you prefer something more physical, allow yourself a few seconds of aimless movement. Stand up and take a couple of steps down the hallway, gazing out the window without searching for anything in particular. Breathe and notice the sounds around you—maybe the hum of a computer or distant chatter. Or if you can, stretch your arms, lengthening your spine like a sleepy cat: this small stretch can release tension trapped in your muscles.

You don't need much time—one or two minutes between commitments is enough. The goal isn't to transform every pause into a long meditation session, but to introduce tiny pockets of awareness into your day. These micro-pauses, repeated consistently, teach your mind that it doesn't have to run nonstop. Over time, you'll feel the need for these intervals of calm, as if they were appointments with yourself. You'll notice that your concentration improves and your mood benefits.

The real challenge isn't to find a free hour, but to learn to fit these breaks into your daily flow. Just a few seconds can reconnect you with your body, your senses, with the simple fact of being here now. It's a gift you give yourself: reclaiming a moment of tranquility even when the day seems reluctant to grant you any.

## Listening to Your Body's Signals

How many times have you ignored a slight physical discomfort, thinking, "It'll pass on its own; I don't have time for this nonsense"? Maybe you carried on studying, playing sports, or working until that minor tension grew into a more serious ache. Your body is constantly communicating: it can send signals of tiredness, stress, a need for movement or rest. Often, caught up in the frenzy of goals and obligations, we fail to stop and listen.

To start, don't just notice when something hurts. At least once a day, try "mapping" your body from head to toe: close your eyes and, starting from your scalp, move slowly downward, paying attention to each area, looking for tension but also neutral or pleasant sensations. Maybe you find your shoulders a bit stiff, but the feel of your clothes on your skin is comfortable. Or your forehead might be relaxed while your hands are cold. This exercise isn't about judging; it's about acknowledging how you feel. It's a way to create an internal dialogue based on observation, not criticism.

If you detect a tight spot, instead of ignoring it, take a small action: stand up, walk a bit, gently massage the back of your neck or your temples with your fingertips, or rotate your shoulders to loosen the knot that's formed. If your eyes feel tired, look away from your book or screen for a few seconds, focusing on a distant point. Even drinking a glass of water with full awareness can restore a tiny balance. The idea isn't to spend hours pampering yourself, but to insert tiny gestures of care that, over time, make a difference.

At the same time, don't wait for pain to force you to pay attention. If you learn to recognize subtle signals—like a faint discomfort in your neck before it turns into a stiff neck—you can prevent bigger problems. No need to be alarmist: if you feel a slight tingle in your lower back, move around or find a more comfortable position. If your legs feel worn out, a minute of gentle stretching can re-energize you. By doing these small things daily, you stop treating your body as a mere vehicle and start seeing it as an ally informing you of your inner state.

Over time, you'll become more skilled at deciphering these signals. You'll know when a break is needed, when a deep breath suffices, when it's time to reorganize your study space for better ergonomics. This harmony with your body improves the quality of your days, helping you work, study, and live with more comfort and clarity. Instead of ending the day exhausted and sore, you'll have interacted with your body, preventing bigger issues before they arise. It's an act of self-care, a form of respect for the equilibrium that allows you to stay active, focused, and ready to seize opportunities.

## Establishing a Nurturing Routine for Your Mind

Think of a routine as a small garden you tend to every day. You don't have to plant giant trees; a few flowers, a bit of moss, a small aromatic herb will do. In the same way, a nurturing routine for your mind doesn't require grand gestures: it's made of simple, personalized actions that, repeated consistently, create a welcoming habitat in your inner life.

For example, rather than just taking a deep breath now and then, you could design a mini morning ritual: as soon as you wake up, play a song that brings you calm and listen to it for a minute without doing anything else. Or slowly sip a glass of water, imagining you're also

94

"hydrating" your mind, preparing it to face the day. If you love to write, dedicate five minutes to a personal notebook—not just to vent your thoughts, but to observe small progress from week to week. Maybe yesterday you felt more anxious, and today you feel more balanced; noting this change makes your growth tangible.

Personalization is key. If you enjoy drawing but aren't very good at it, no problem: allow yourself a couple of minutes to doodle abstract shapes, letting your hand move as if dancing without an audience. If music relaxes you, create a short playlist of three or four songs to listen to at specific times of the day, like a "soundtrack" that stabilizes your mood. If you're passionate about nature, keep a small plant on your desk and give it a thoughtful glance whenever you feel overwhelmed, acknowledging that as you study, the plant grows quietly, unhurried.

These routines aren't tasks to check off a list, but seeds you plant with care. There's no final evaluation; no one will ask you to grade your "mindfulness session." If you skip a day, try again tomorrow. What matters is creating a thread that connects different moments in your inner life, giving them continuity. Over time, you'll notice that when the outside world becomes noisy, you have a reference point: you know you can return to your ritual, your morning song, or your notebook, and rediscover some balance.

This approach makes self-care constant and gentle, not a bitter medicine taken only in emergencies. As these routines become steady, you'll recognize the difference between a day when you've dedicated yourself to these gestures and one when you haven't. It's not about perfection, but about presence: a mind nourished by small, attentive acts becomes more flexible, more serene, ready to face challenges with a deeper breath. And that's a victory you can renew every day, in your own way.

# Chapter 13:
# Celebrate Your Individuality

*"Comparison is the thief of joy." – Theodore Roosevelt*

Have you ever felt that subtle tightening in your chest when you see someone who seems to have something you don't? It doesn't matter if it's a success, a physical trait, or a natural talent: sometimes just a moment is enough to make you feel like you're racing in a contest that isn't yours. And yet, chasing someone else's ideal often drains energy instead of motivating you to grow. This chapter aims to guide you away from constant comparisons, showing how to transform envy into a chance for reflection, and eventually rediscover the value of your own uniqueness. It's about learning to look inward with kinder eyes, recognizing that your individuality doesn't depend on measuring yourself against someone else.

## Freeing Yourself from Silent Envy

Think about that subtle tension you feel when you see someone achieve a goal you'd like for yourself. Maybe a classmate who lands an important role in a project, or a friend who seems to pick up a foreign language with impressive ease. Silent envy isn't a monster to fight off with anger, but a signal to interpret. Instead of letting it become a sterile comparison, you can turn it into a reason for personal growth.

Let's try a practical exercise: recall a recent situation in which you felt envy. Pick a specific episode—perhaps when you saw someone post about a sports achievement or display a certificate of academic merit. Write down the scene and describe what you felt: irritation, a sense of lack, fear of not measuring up. Then ask yourself: what exactly struck me in that situation? Was it the other person's diligence, their confidence, their steady effort, or their ability to manage their time?

Now, rather than letting envy remain a feeling of discomfort, use it as a clue. If you envied someone's ease with public speaking, ask how you could improve your own speaking skills. Maybe sign up for a small theater workshop, or practice each week by speaking aloud on a topic you care about, recording yourself with your phone and reviewing the videos to track progress. This way, envy becomes a direction to invest your energy in, instead of a weight that drags you down.

Try to demystify the other person's accomplishment: often we only see the end result, not the road traveled to get there. That triumph might be the fruit of months of hard work, hidden failures, and moments of doubt. Realizing that behind every success lies a process makes envy less sharp and more human. It reminds you that you too can undertake a similar journey, in your own time and manner.

Also, cultivate gratitude for what you already have. Make a list of your strengths, even small ones: the ability to organize your study time, good relationships with classmates, or cooking a tasty dish. When envy creeps in, look at this list—not to convince yourself you're better than anyone, but to remember that your life isn't empty, and what you have is genuinely valuable. This reduces the sense of "something missing."

In the end, envy can transform from a silent enemy into a useful signal. You don't need to ignore it or punish yourself for feeling it. Welcome it, analyze it, and ask what it's telling you. Then act, setting concrete goals to improve in that direction without trying to copy anyone else. Envy becomes a stimulus to better understand yourself and invest in what truly matters to you. Freeing yourself from envy doesn't mean making it disappear entirely; it means using it as leverage for self-knowledge and growth.

## Recognizing Your Own Uniqueness

Have you ever considered that some of your strengths might be so subtle that no one ever openly praises them? Perhaps you always remember everyone's birthdays, or you have a reassuring tone of voice when a friend is anxious. Maybe you're great at creating the perfect playlist for any mood, or arranging your desk to be both cozy and functional. Recognizing your own uniqueness means bringing these "invisible" qualities to the surface.

We often focus on "spotlight" talents: singing beautifully, excelling in a sport, or having flawless grades. But uniqueness isn't just about that. It's formed by the sum of both big and small abilities: being patient while solving complicated puzzles, sensing when someone needs personal space, being creative in finding fun ways to spend time, or having the sensitivity to pick up on others' emotions. All these nuances, even if quiet, hold value.

Try this exercise: write a list of three or four traits that belong to you but rarely get noticed. They can be quirky or subtle strengths. For example: "I stay calm when everyone around me is stressed," "I can make my friends smile with a short, funny story," or "I notice when someone is feeling down even if they don't say it." Once on paper, these qualities don't seem trivial anymore. They become little gems in your personal collection.

Remember that your uniqueness evolves: new experiences, interests, and relationships enrich it over time. If you used to be terrified of public speaking and now you can manage it without too much anxiety, that marks an evolution in your unique profile. Don't think of your identity as a fixed label, but as a painting that's constantly changing. The more you get to know yourself, the more you expand the range of hues that define you.

Recognizing your uniqueness doesn't mean downplaying that of others. It's like admiring a garden: every flower has its own color and shape. There's no need to decide which is the most beautiful; the richness lies in the variety. So when comparison tries to creep in, remind yourself that you don't have to compete to prove you're special. You already are, in your own natural way, even in those small things you do effortlessly.

Ultimately, recognizing your own uniqueness is an act of self-love. It lets you view your journey not through the lens of constant self-criticism, but with the openness of someone discovering precious details within themselves. This makes the urge to compare yourself with someone "better" or "worse" less pressing: you have your colors, others have theirs. There's no absolute hierarchy, just a collection of unique individuals making the world more varied and interesting.

## Embracing Others' Successes with Serenity

Think about the last time you saw someone close to you achieve something important. Maybe a classmate who won a competition, a friend who got a scholarship, or an acquaintance who passed a difficult exam. If you felt a mix of joy and a slight twinge of discomfort, don't feel guilty: it's human. But if you want to prevent that feeling from turning bitter, you can adopt a more constructive approach.

Instead of just thinking "Lucky them," try a practical exercise: when you witness someone else's success, take a minute to write down two things. First: what aspect of that success impresses you the most (consistency, creativity, patience)? Second: how can you draw inspiration from that quality to improve a small area of your own life? For example, if your friend earned recognition for an artistic project and you envy her skill, you could decide to spend 15 minutes a day exploring a creative activity that intrigues you, without worrying about the outcome. This turns observing someone else's success into a positive reframing: no longer a threat, but a spark for your own growth.

You can also keep a mini-journal of others' accomplishments. Not to compare yourself, but to remind yourself that the world is full of diverse achievements. Note when someone reaches an interesting goal, write down what you can learn from it. At the end of the week, review these notes and ask yourself if there's something you can integrate into your routine or approach. This way, you see other people's successes as part of a wide, multifaceted landscape where no single model of achievement dominates.

Expressing genuine appreciation can strengthen relationships. Don't hold back a heartfelt "Congratulations, you worked hard and it shows!" Being able to celebrate others' victories without resentment creates a supportive environment. And when your moment comes, you'll find people ready to do the same for you. Embracing others' successes calmly is not only a gift to yourself but a seed planted in your relationships, making them more fertile for understanding and solidarity.

Remember: welcoming others' successes with serenity doesn't reduce your merit or limit your potential. On the contrary, it shows you that you're not in competition with the whole world. Personal growth isn't measured by comparisons, but by the goals you choose to pursue based on your own inclinations. Seeing others achieve results can inspire you to look for new paths without taking anything away from your own journey. Instead of feeling threatened, you can draw inspiration, building a more open and confident mindset.

**Valuing Your Distinctive Voice**

Recall an occasion when you wanted to express a differing opinion but hesitated. Maybe during a heated debate among friends, or in a classroom discussion where everyone seemed to agree except you. Valuing your distinctive voice doesn't mean shouting louder than everyone else, but rather creating a space where your opinion can emerge clearly and respectfully.

You can adopt a simple "protocol" for these situations. First step: prepare mentally before speaking. Think of a polite introductory phrase like, "I'd like to offer a slightly different perspective." This way, you don't come across as aggressive, but announce your intention to contribute in a collaborative tone. Second step: focus on one aspect of the topic instead of multiple points at once. Choose what you find most important, so you don't dilute your message's impact. Third step: present your idea without expecting universal approval. Remind yourself that not everyone will agree, and that's okay. Your goal isn't to convince everyone, but to let your voice be heard. Consider others' reactions as feedback, not a verdict. If someone responds constructively, listen, take notes, and see if you can refine or clarify your point. If another person reacts negatively, it doesn't mean you're wrong; perhaps their resistance stems from fear of change or simple habit.

Another tip: look for potential allies. If you think a classmate or a friend might share your viewpoint, mention it to them beforehand. Knowing you're not the only "dissenting" voice can give you confidence. But even if you stand alone, your voice has value as an expression of your individuality, experiences, and sensitivities. Finally, don't view every exchange as a duel. If someone disagrees, you're not defeated. Often, differing ideas lead to new insights and fresh perspectives. By hearing your viewpoint, others might discover an overlooked element. And by hearing their objections, you might strengthen or refine your reasoning. Valuing your distinctive voice is a process in which you learn not to vanish into silence, not to give up on your ideas out of fear of judgment. Over time, you'll feel more comfortable expressing even unconventional thoughts. You'll remember that differing opinions don't ruin harmony—they enrich it. And you, with your voice, add a new note to the chorus, making it more complete. Being yourself, even when you're in the minority, is a gift both to you and to those who listen.

# Chapter 14:
# Cultivating Gratitude

*"Gratitude turns what we have into enough." – Aesop*

Imagine opening your eyes on a typical morning, your head still half-immersed in dreams, your body craving a few more minutes under the covers. Before even getting up, your mind is already catching hold of the day's to-do list: a test at school, a message you haven't answered yet, a commitment you can't postpone. You might feel a subtle sense of pressure, as if the day is already demanding too much. Yet, in that very moment, you have a chance: find even the smallest reason to feel grateful. Maybe it's a ray of sunlight warming the floor through the window, the smell of coffee someone just brewed in the kitchen, or the memory of a quiet conversation with someone dear to you the night before. In that brief moment of focus, without any grand effort, the tension eases just a bit.

## Discovering Little Gifts... in Real Time

Think of your day as a continuous film: scenes passing by, conversations, colors, and sounds you might never truly notice. Have you ever tried to appreciate a single frame the moment it appears? Instead of waiting until the end of the day to mentally review what happened, try something different: catch these "small gifts" as they appear, even if it's just for a few seconds.

We're not talking about a structured ritual or a formal exercise. Imagine you're in the school hallway, between classes, and you notice a fleeting smile exchanged between two classmates. In that instant, think: "This is a small gift, a tiny note of harmony." Or you're waiting at the bus stop, listening to the wind in the trees, and you realize that this sound feels soothing: there's another gift, captured right as it happens.

The idea isn't to dive into lengthy reflections but to develop a reflex: the reflex of recognizing a pleasant sensation, a kind gesture, or an unexpected detail right when you experience it. It's like tasting delicious food and savoring it immediately, without waiting until the end of the meal to say, "That was good." This approach makes gratitude a discreet travel companion, always ready to get your attention when something positive passes before your eyes or stimulates your senses.

And if you're worried about forgetting these moments, don't be. There's no need to jot them down or formalize them in an evening list. The point is to learn to recognize them "in real time," so that your mind gets used to spotting flashes of beauty or kindness in your normal routine. Over time, you'll naturally notice more of what you used to overlook. The strength of this method lies in its spontaneity: it doesn't ask you to pause later, but to catch the moment as it flows.

Whether it's an encouraging word spoken on the fly, the reflection of light on a puddle, or the scent of a cake baking in the oven, every moment can become a tiny source of gratitude. You don't have to prepare, wait for the right time, or require absolute silence. You just need the willingness to tell yourself: "Here's a little gift, right now, right here."

As time goes on, this habit will help you build a richer perception of your day. You won't need to wait until evening to anxiously search for positive memories: you'll have gathered many along the way. Gratitude thus becomes a constantly active radar, capable of detecting pleasant signals amid the everyday hustle. Not a structured exercise, but a more alert and open way of living.

In the end, learning to appreciate these little gifts in real time means choosing not to let positive details pass unnoticed. It means saying to the world: "I see you, and even though not everything is perfect, these moments are worth acknowledging."

## Turning Challenges into an Appreciation of Your Resources

When you face an obstacle—a disappointment, an unexpected event, or a result below your expectations—it's natural to feel discouraged. But instead of focusing on "downsizing" the problem to make it less overwhelming (a concept you've already seen in chapters about stress), let's try a different perspective. It's not just about seeing the problem as smaller, but using it to highlight the resources you already have, even in the midst of difficulty.

Think of a situation where something went wrong: a test didn't go well, you argued with a friend, or a project didn't yield the results you hoped for. Rather than asking yourself how to reduce its emotional impact (which you already know how to handle with techniques learned elsewhere), ask yourself: "What abilities or strengths do I have that can help me face this situation?" Maybe you're good at adapting, or you know someone who can give you helpful advice. Maybe, despite the disappointment, you're determined to improve, or you have past experience guiding you through similar moments.

In this context, gratitude serves as a reminder that you're never without tools. Even if you've met a challenge, you're not starting from scratch. You have qualities, relationships, knowledge, and small achievements that no failure can erase. Shift your focus away from the problem's size and onto the quality of your resources. It's not about denying the difficulty, but recognizing that you're better equipped than you think.

For example, if you got a low grade, rather than dwelling only on how serious the mistake is, remember that you've made progress in other subjects or that in the past you managed to fill gaps through persistence. If a friend let you down, don't just brood over the hurt: acknowledge your courage in facing the situation, your capacity to seek clarification, or the fact that you have other people you can rely on.

This perspective turns the problem into an opportunity to reassess what you've already built within and around you. Every obstacle becomes a mirror that, besides reflecting the difficulty, also shows glimpses of your skills, resilience, network of relationships, or lessons you've already learned. It's a way of never feeling stripped bare in the face of setbacks, because you can always draw on a reserve of experiences and support that gratitude helps you appreciate.

With this approach, gratitude isn't just about calming yourself down; it's about reminding you that, even in the midst of a challenge, you're not empty-handed. You know you possess a set of resources you can rely on, and this changes how you perceive and handle difficulties. Not just "reducing the problem," but "recognizing your strength."

## Changing How You Experience Relationships, Not the Environment

Gratitude doesn't just influence how you perceive your successes or hardships; it also plays a role in how you interpret your relationships. However, you don't have to imagine a chain reaction that transforms your entire social circle, nor expect miracles in the mindset of those around you. Instead, gratitude works like an internal lens that modifies your approach to interactions, helping you see what happens between you and others without idealizing or demonizing the outside world.

Picture a simple conversation. Before cultivating gratitude, you might enter that dialogue with a mind full of expectations, fears, or suspicions. A neutral comment could seem like a judgment, a suggestion might sound like criticism. By training yourself to spot even small positive aspects in your life, you change how you interpret external stimuli. A classmate's remark feels less threatening if your overall perspective includes reassuring reference points and reasons to appreciate who you are and what you have.

It's not about becoming naïve or seeing only the good. On the contrary, gratitude makes you more clear-headed. With a stock of positive elements to draw from (memories of kind gestures, awareness of your own skills, recent moments of serenity), you no longer start from an emotional deficit. This lets you evaluate each human exchange more fairly. If someone offers constructive feedback, rather than feeling attacked, you can consider the context, ask yourself whether there's something useful in their words, or whether the intention might have been helpful rather than hurtful. At the same time, if you encounter someone genuinely negative, gratitude helps ensure that one bad encounter doesn't overshadow everything else, reminding you that there are other people and other situations that balance out that unpleasant moment.

In short, gratitude allows you to navigate social dynamics more calmly. You're not trying to change others or make your environment perfect; you're improving your ability to read situations. If previously a minor misunderstanding could make you doubt your worth, now you don't take it as a final judgment—because you've learned you already have reasons to feel stable and confident. If a friend helps you out, you don't take it for granted or view it as a sign of your weakness. Instead, you see it as a moment of genuine collaboration.

Ultimately, gratitude doesn't magically create a better world, but it gives you a more reliable compass to move through the real world, with real people who can be complex or contradictory. This compass helps you stay on course in your relationships without feeling at the mercy of others' moods or circumstances, turning each encounter into an opportunity for understanding, calm, and maturity.

## Using Gratitude to Navigate Daily Decisions

After learning to recognize the small gifts in everyday life, discovering a method to put problems into perspective, and understanding how gratitude can influence your interpretation of relationships, it's time to consider how this attitude can guide the countless choices you make continuously, often without even realizing it. Here, we're not talking about big future plans or long-term goals—those are addressed elsewhere in this book—but about the small decisions that weave together the fabric of your daily life.

Think about the many minor decisions that fill a typical day: how to respond to a snide comment, whether to accept a last-minute invitation, what to read before bed, how to handle a small setback, or which friends you should spend time with. Taken individually, these choices may seem trivial, but combined, they shape your mood, your energy level, and your sense of living a life aligned with your values.

In these situations, gratitude can serve as an emotional filter, a lens that helps you interpret each scenario more calmly. For example, if someone makes a cutting remark, instead of snapping back instantly, you can pause and remind yourself of a few positive aspects of your environment: maybe you're lucky enough to be in a place where you can freely express yourself, or you've experienced supportive relationships that show not all interactions are tense. This brief moment of gratitude doesn't erase the annoyance, but it prevents you from reacting solely out of irritation and gives you room for a more thoughtful response.

Similarly, when you face a seemingly neutral choice—like how to spend a break or which activity to pick for relaxation—gratitude encourages you to consider what truly nourishes you mentally and emotionally. Instead of choosing the most convenient option or the one that habitually draws you in, ask yourself: "Right now, what would make me feel more appreciative of my day?" Maybe it's a short walk outside, sending a thank-you message to someone you care about, or taking a few minutes to read an inspiring book.

Gratitude, then, isn't just a feeling to cultivate when everything is going well; it's a tool you can engage strategically, almost like an internal compass. Rather than passively enduring circumstances, you choose to interpret them knowing that your life isn't defined solely by shortcomings and tension, but also by resources, constructive encounters, and moments of calm. This doesn't mean looking at the world through rose-colored glasses, but acknowledging that you carry within you a set of positive experiences you can draw upon when needed.

Over time, using gratitude to navigate daily decisions will become second nature. As you mentally sift through your options, you'll instinctively consider the one that best aligns with feelings of appreciation and serenity already present in your life. In this way, without grand proclamations or complicated strategies, you'll gradually transform your daily life into a more coherent, peaceful, and profoundly enriching tapestry.

# Chapter 15:
# Shaping the Future: Dreams, Goals, and Actions

*"All our dreams can come true, if we have the courage to pursue them." – Walt Disney*

Imagine closing your eyes for a moment. Picture the life you want in a few years: maybe you see yourself in a place you love, surrounded by people who make you feel good, or immersed in activities that today seem like a distant horizon. Perhaps that future appears blurry, or maybe it's already quite clear. In any case, the central question is: how can you move from mere desire to a genuinely achievable goal? This chapter will guide you toward turning your dreams into concrete objectives, showing you how to give your ambitions a more tangible shape.

It's not about making impossible lists or forcing yourself to chase ideals that aren't yours. Rather, it's an invitation to explore what truly matters to you, to recognize the authentic desires that can motivate you even when the road gets tough. After all, it's common to feel confused by the vastness of the future: you might have many ideas but not know where to begin, or believe you lack the ability or resources. Often, what's missing isn't talent, but a method to outline step-by-step paths, a structure that makes dreams less hazy and more accessible.

This chapter will offer some tools for moving from "I want" to "I can do it," and from "I can do it" to "I'm already starting." It's a crucial shift in your personal growth journey: don't just imagine a perfect picture, learn to build it piece by piece. When a dream takes form, it becomes a goal; when a goal is backed by a plan of action, it begins to come to life in reality.

## Giving Shape to Your Personal Ambitions

Imagine you have a handful of scattered wishes in your mind: maybe you'd like to learn to play an instrument, improve your grasp of a certain subject, or develop a skill that opens new doors. Often these dreams stay vague, as if you're afraid to spell them out. But as long as they remain undefined, they risk never finding a real path.

Start with a simple question: "What does my goal look like, exactly?" If you want to become more independent in your studies, what does that mean? Managing your time better, finding resources on your own, truly understanding concepts without relying on others' notes? If you want to improve in a sport, what level do you aspire to? Do you want to participate in a competition, reach a certain time, or execute a sequence of moves with precision?

Giving shape to your ambitions means turning your desires into a clear image. Write down your wish, then describe it in detail. Don't just say "I want to learn a foreign language": specify which language, what level of proficiency you aim for—casual conversation while traveling, reading books, engaging in professional discussions—and how soon you'd like to see progress. This clarity turns a fleeting thought into a well-defined target, something your mind can start taking seriously.

As you outline these details, also ask yourself why this goal appeals to you. Sometimes there's a deeper need behind a desire: maybe you want to learn a musical instrument not just to play songs, but because you believe this skill can offer a new means of expression, help you relax, and give you a creative outlet. Understanding your internal motivations makes the goal more solid; it's not just a passing whim but something rooted in your vision of the future.

You don't need an endless list of details, just enough to distinguish your goal from a vague "I'd like to." Now you're no longer saying "I want to do better in school," but "I want to raise my average grades to a certain level by the end of the term, learning to revise more efficiently and take more effective notes." With this level of precision, you stop drifting in "maybe" and begin moving towards "I can try this approach."

Once you've defined your ambitions, you'll see them as small projects rather than abstract ideas. Every future decision—what resources to consult, how much time to invest, which tools to use—will find a clear reference point. Giving shape to personal ambitions is like taking a lump of clay that represents your desires and starting to sculpt it, so you don't end up with a shapeless mass of intentions, but something you can truly begin to mold step by step.

## Defining an Actionable Plan

You've set a clear goal, and now you want to make it tangible. Without an action plan, you risk scattering your efforts on random attempts, ending up feeling confused and uncertain. Imagine studying for a challenging exam: if you review topics haphazardly, hopping from one subject to another, you finish unsure of what you've actually covered. On the other hand, if you decide that today you'll tackle two chapters, tomorrow a written exercise, and the day after tomorrow a revision of key concepts, you'll have a neat, less intimidating roadmap.

To build your plan, break your main objective into smaller, concrete sub-goals. If you want to learn a language, don't think about fluency right away. Start with a basic vocabulary set this week, then spend a few days practicing listening with short dialogues, and later move on to simple reading material. Each clearly defined step lets you see progress: you no longer view the goal as a massive block, but as a sequence of manageable steps.

Set approximate deadlines. They're not cages, just time markers. If you aim to complete a certain portion of work in two weeks, in fourteen days you'll look back and see what you've accomplished. If you realize you've underestimated the complexity, you can adjust the timeframe next time. Having a date in mind prevents you from drifting aimlessly. A goal without a date feels like an idea floating in emptiness, while a timeframe anchors it in reality.

Plan for intermediate check-ins. Every so often, pause and ask yourself if you're following the outline. Have you covered the planned material? Have unexpected obstacles arisen? This evaluation isn't a punitive self-exam but a useful dialogue. If you notice delays or skipped steps, it's better to know now, so you can proceed more wisely.

Varying activities helps avoid boredom. If you always follow the same pattern, your mind grows dull. Alternate between more intense sessions and lighter ones, experiment with different learning methods, try rearranging the order of tasks. Even a small tweak keeps your mind alert. You're not a machine repeating the same sequence endlessly; you can make your learning or training path more vibrant.

Track your progress. Checking off a completed sub-goal, noting what you've finished, or seeing a list of accomplished tasks provides immediate satisfaction. This awareness of what you've already done reminds you that you're not stuck at the starting point. Each checkmark is like a tiny trophy, concrete proof that you're moving forward.

A well-organized plan doesn't trap you; it guides you. Without it, you might waste time on minor parts while neglecting what's crucial. With a reference map, you proceed more confidently. You have timelines, stages, variations, mid-course checks, and a log of achievements. You've brought your goal closer to reality, turning it from a hazy dream into a set of tangible steps.

## Sustaining Motivation on Sluggish Days

Some mornings you might wake up feeling less energetic, as if your drive slipped away overnight. Motivation can fluctuate, sometimes for no clear reason. Maybe you slept poorly, maybe yesterday you didn't finish what you'd planned, or perhaps you can't yet see tangible results. These feelings are normal; motivation doesn't remain steady. What matters is learning how to spark it even when it doesn't arise spontaneously.

First, recall the deeper reason behind your choice. If you're investing in a skill that will offer more career freedom, imagine the satisfaction of not being limited by certain conditions. If you're working on physical fitness, envision the lightness, the confidence in your body, the extra energy you'll have each day. This broader sense of purpose acts as a light on dull days: you're not just struggling, you're building a solid foundation for the future.

If monotony dries out your enthusiasm, change the atmosphere. If you're studying a language, include short videos, fun audio clips, or interaction with real people. If you're training physically, try different exercises, experiment with new intensities or complementary activities. Small changes can break the mental dullness that makes each effort heavy. A tiny shift in scenario can renew your interest.

Reward yourself for partial achievements. Don't wait until the end of the journey to acknowledge progress. If you've completed a study module, passed a small test, or improved since last week, give yourself a treat. Maybe a free afternoon, a chat with a friend about your progress, or a small symbolic purchase. These gestures show that your efforts yield something concrete, even if not definitive, fueling forward momentum.

Seek support from others. One piece of practical advice, a success story from someone who overcame similar difficulties, or a shared laugh over a minor mishap can bring fresh perspectives. You're not isolated in your effort; knowing that others have navigated similar hurdles reveals opportunities you hadn't considered.

Observe your emotional responses without judging yourself. If you feel frustrated, acknowledge it. You don't have to force artificial enthusiasm. Motivation is a seed that can grow if you give it space to breathe. There will be less brilliant days, but even the grayest experience can teach you how to rekindle what feels lost. You're not failing because you feel less driven today; you're simply experiencing a different phase. Understanding these fluctuations will give you tools to revive your motivation over time.

## Reflecting Your Values in Everyday Actions

Ask yourself which principles you'd like your choices to embody. It's not about comparing final results with inner satisfaction, but about considering each step you take. If cooperation matters to you, find ways to interact with others—share knowledge, offer mutual support. If transparency is important, avoid shady shortcuts: choosing ethical resources, clear strategies, and small honest gestures gives your efforts deeper meaning.

Picture a learning journey: you can approach it quickly and mechanically, or you can select materials, texts, and methods that spark your curiosity—one of your core values. In doing so, you're not just accumulating words or skills, you're fostering an open mind. If empathy guides you, dedicate time to those who struggle, offering advice or constructive exchanges. Each act reflects the person you want to be, not just a means to gain competence.

If you sense a mismatch between your methods and what you consider important, treat that feeling as a signal, not a reason for discouragement. Maybe you picked a dry, impersonal resource just to speed things up and now feel unsatisfied. This discomfort suggests adjusting your approach. Perhaps slow down, pay more attention to the depth of content or the quality of the relationships formed along the way. You don't have to overhaul everything overnight; small adjustments align your actions with what feels true.

You don't need grand declarations or dramatic gestures. Often it's about subtle nuances: opting for more thoughtful study materials, being attentive not to overshadow someone less experienced, avoiding harsh demands on yourself that clash with your sense of balance. These details add depth to your journey, making it more than a routine accumulation of effort.

If you realize a certain goal, while useful, doesn't resonate with your values, consider rethinking priorities. It's not surrender, it's growth. You're learning who you are through what you choose to do daily. Don't just complete tasks: let them reflect your idea of integrity, your idea of respect, your idea of humanity. Thus, you're not merely collecting results; you're defining the person you become with every step you take.

## Thank You for Sharing This Journey

Dear reader,

I hope this book has inspired you and helped you see how strong and capable you are of creating the life you deserve. The journey toward self-love isn't always easy, but every step you take is a gift to yourself.

If you feel enriched by the experience of this book, I'd like to invite you to share your thoughts by leaving a review. It doesn't matter whether it's positive or negative—what matters is that it's honest. Your words can help other girls like you discover a new way of looking at themselves, embracing who they are, and believing in their potential.

As an author, your feedback means so much to me. I personally read every review, and your input helps me continue creating content that can truly make a difference.

Thank you for your time and support.

Warmly,

Grace Parker

Scan to leave a review on Amazon if
you live in the US

Scan to leave a review on
Amazon if you live in the UK

Scan to leave a review on Amazon
if you live in Canada

Scan to leave a review on
Amazon if you live in Australia

# Conclusion

Imagine that not too long ago, you realized you no longer recognized yourself in the choices you were making. Perhaps you felt pulled by outside pressures, maybe your inner voice judged every step, or maybe you were chasing goals that didn't feel truly yours. From these reflections, you explored practical tools, learning how to shape authentic objectives, build actionable plans, and find support in more genuine relationships. You learned to view reality with sharper focus, to reduce the impact of unfair judgments, to nurture motivation even when the path seemed uphill, to infuse the journey with renewed meaning. Step by step, you realized you don't need to be perfect, just authentic; you don't need to please everyone, just respect who you are; you don't have to copy imposed models, just listen to your curiosity, inner strength, and values.

At this point, you've gathered a set of ideas, reflections, and examples that can truly make a difference in your daily life. Don't let them slip away like water through your fingers. Take action, experiment, even if it's just changing a single detail in your routine tomorrow. Test out one small strategy you learned here: pause a few seconds before saying "yes" to an invitation that doesn't feel right, or take a moment at the end of the day to acknowledge a small success, or open your notebook of priorities and check if it really reflects what matters to you.

Your journey doesn't end on the last page. Each piece of advice you've read is like a seed: it can germinate if you plant it in soil enriched by courage and trust. Don't fear imperfect attempts. Every attempt, even a clumsy one, brings you closer to a more self-aware version of yourself. If you encounter obstacles, remember that mistakes don't define you. You've seen how even dark moments can provide unexpected lessons, revealing resources you never suspected you had.

As the author, I want to leave you with a heartfelt thought. I'm grateful for the time you devoted to these pages, for your curiosity, and for your desire to grow. Every topic we touched on now belongs to you: use it to create spaces of serenity, to cultivate more honest relationships, to choose goals that resonate with the person you want to become. Don't wait for ideal circumstances. Start now, with what you have at hand, with the emotions and ideas you carry in your heart.

I hope you move forward with a light step and an open mind, unafraid of change and ready to embrace every bit of progress as a sign that you're building something authentic. You've learned effective strategies, reflected on your priorities, and imagined new scenarios. Now is the time to put them into practice. Good luck on your journey: may your determination guide you toward a future rich in meaning.

# About the Author

Grace Parker is a passionate advocate for personal growth and self-love. With a special focus on the unique challenges faced by teenage girls, Grace is dedicated to providing practical tools and inspiring messages to help them overcome insecurities, build inner confidence, and live authentically.

Having grown up in an environment where societal expectations often overshadowed emotional well-being, Grace embarked on her own journey to rediscover her self-worth and break free from the cycle of seeking external validation. This experience inspired her to share what she's learned, offering young women guidance on embracing self-awareness and creating a fulfilling and genuine life.

With a direct and engaging style, Grace encourages her readers to look within, embrace themselves unconditionally, and craft a life that reflects their dreams and aspirations. When she's not writing, Grace enjoys exploring nature, practicing yoga, and nurturing her love for art and music.

For Grace, self-love isn't just a topic—it's a mission: to help the next generation recognize their potential and live with confidence and gratitude.

www.ingramcontent.com/pod-product-compliance
Lightning Source LLC
Chambersburg PA
CBHW070503090426
42735CB00012B/2660